Life after Youth

Making Sense of One Man's Journey through the Transition at Mid-life

D0067303

Sean D. Sammon, FMS

ALBA·HOUSE   NEW·YORK

SOCIETY OF ST. PAUL, 2187 VICTORY BLVD., STATEN ISLAND, NEW YORK 10314

ST PAULS

Library of Congress Cataloging-in-Publication Data

Sammon, Sean D.
    Life after youth: making sense of one man's journey through the
transition at mid-life / Sean D. Sammon.
        p.   cm.
    Includes bibliographical references.
    ISBN 0-8189-0778-9
    1. Middle-aged men — Psychology. 2. Midlife crisis. 3. Maturation
(Psychology) 4. Developmental psychology. 5. Spiritual life.
6. Monastic and religious life. I. Title.
HQ1059.4.S35   1997
305.244 — dc21   96-49472
                                                CIP

Produced and designed in the United States of America by the
Fathers and Brothers of the Society of St. Paul,
2187 Victory Boulevard, Staten Island, New York 10314,
as part of their communications apostolate.

ISBN: 0-8189-0778-9

Printing Information:

Current Printing - first digit	1	2	3	4	5	6	7	8	9	10

Year of Current Printing - first year shown

1997	1998	1999	2000	2001	2002	2003	2004	2005

1. Life After Youth

LIFE AFTER YOUTH

DEDICATION

To John Perring-Mulligan —
mentor, friend, and brother

CONTENTS

INTRODUCTION

*O*n January 21st, 1994, after several weeks of extensive medical testing, I was diagnosed with a brain tumor. Hardly welcome news. At age 46 my world turned upside down suddenly as I moved quickly from person to patient. The endocrinologist's startling words are as clear today as they were when she first spoke them: "You have a tumor in the pituitary area. It is extensive: five centimeters in diameter. We will use medication to shrink the tissue, but you cannot avoid neurosurgery." After a pause, she added, "It's benign." "Great," I thought, "every cloud does have its silver lining!" Seven weeks later I was wheeled into the operating room of a New York hospital for a procedure that lasted more than five hours.

In July of the same year, on the first of the month, a friend and fellow Marist Brother, Chris Mannion, was killed by troops of the Rwandan Patriotic Front in Save, Rwanda. Chris was in the country working to free a number of men and women religious who were being detained by the then existing government. Also involved in the rescue effort and murdered along with Chris that day was another Brother of mine, Joseph Rushigajiki. Their deaths followed the tragic slaying in April

1994 of four more of my Marist Brothers by government and militia forces: Fabien Bisengimana, Gaspard Gatali, Pierre Canisius Nyilinkindi and Etienne Rwesa, and the assassination of Brother Henri Verges in Algeria in May by Islamic extremists.

One year later, in July 1995, a telephone call brought news that, for the third time in about a dozen years, cancer had come into the life of yet another friend. Breda had battled this dread disease with courage and dignity twice before. This time, though, resignation was among the emotions reflected in her voice. That fact made me wonder initially whether she had the strength and will to do the same once again. Thankfully, her fighting spirit returned within a few weeks. While still not sure of her long term prognosis, with the help of prayer and medical science, she is fighting the good fight.

In the midst of all of the above, I moved from the United States to Rome, Italy to take up a new work for my Institute. Having been elected Vicar General during a 1993 General Chapter, I knew that eight years of administration, planning, and travel lay ahead. Language was the first challenge I faced. All meetings of our General Council and, indeed, a good bit of our life together as a community were to be conducted in French. Lacking any appreciable knowledge of that language, I came quickly to understand what people meant when they said: "You'll feel like a child learning to speak French." A plane trip of just a few hours reduced me from a forty-six-year-old man with an ability to express himself clearly to a two- or three-year-old struggling to communicate even his most basic needs.

Why am I relating all these facts? Quite simply to explain why I wrote this book. The diagnosis of a brain tumor, the death of my friend and Brother, the illness of another friend, and the loss of my country, culture, and language threw me into an unexpected mid-life crisis. Up until that time, I thought I was navigating well the rivers and streams of that predictable transition in adult life. Little did I know what lay in store for me. I wrote this book hoping that the story of my journey through the transition at mid-life might be of help to other men, and perhaps some women too. You will find no answers here, just the experience of one man in his late forties as he tried to make some sense of what was happening to him.

A brain tumor, murder, the return of cancer: are the circumstances triggering a transition at mid-life always so dramatic? Not really. Many of life's more routine events are among the catalysts that get any transition underway: a job change, the beginning or end of a relationship, a move from one city to another, an opportunity for further education, to name but a few. One or all of these developments might be the factor that kick-starts a transition in your own life.

Writing has always provided an emotional release for me; putting some of the details of my mid-life journey down on paper has helped me experience more deeply and understand better the process of conversion that got underway that wintry Friday afternoon in New Rochelle, New York, when the doctor first told me about the brain tumor. Now, almost twenty-four months later, I am surprised at the changes I find in myself. I can also honestly say that while I would not have gone looking for the upheaval of the last two years, I would not have missed any of it for the world.

This book includes several personal essays about my own mid-life transition interspersed with chapters addressing contemporary theory about this fertile time in life. The latter set the subject within the context of developmental psychology and spiritual growth, and offer a brief and general treatment of a wide range of topics commonly associated with mid-life. The book begins with an essay entitled *Mid-life Tumor*; it captures my experience of mid-life illness and sets the tone for what follows. This chapter appeared first as an article in *Review for Religious* (March/April 1995). I'm grateful to David Fleming, SJ and the staff at the *Review* for permission to reprint it. The next chapter, *Life after Youth*, explains some fundamental concepts about adult development; it will help you better understand the mid-life and other transitions.

Chapter III, another personal essay entitled *Mid-life Mortalities*, picks up the theme first introduced in *Mid-life Tumor* but expands it to include a discussion of Chris' death and all the "little deaths" that mid-life brings with it. A chapter entitled *The Transition at Mid-life* follows and addresses directly this important time of growth and its tasks.

Chapter V, *Desert Days*, lays out my reaction to Breda's recurrent cancer. Through her illness, I came to realize that the God I knew earlier in life was hardly God at all. The book's next chapter, *Mid-life and Afterwards*, completes our discussion about middle age and lets the reader peek ahead to the years after mid-life and its transition.

Testosterone Trials follows as Chapter VII. This essay and *Mid-life Athlete*, Chapter IX, address some of the physical and sexual changes that mid-life brought my way. They might touch a different nerve in some mid-life people than the three previous essays. Chapter VIII, *Coping with the Transition at Mid-life*, is sandwiched between these two final essays. It offers some practical advice on how to deal with the changes that mid-life brings.

Reflection questions appear at the end of Chapters II, IV, VI, VIII and IX; they may assist you in making the material in this book your own. When considering each question, take a few quiet minutes alone and jot down some of your thoughts for later reference and, perhaps, discussion with others.

Among other sources, I have used two of my previous books, *Growing Pains in Ministry*, and *An Undivided Heart:*

Making Sense of Celibate Chastity, and an article I wrote, *Life After Youth*, as the basis for the chapters that describe contemporary theory about mid-life. Readers looking for further information about this topic are urged to consult these sources directly. They are referenced in the *Recommended Readings* section in the back of the book. Also included in these chapters are the findings of a number of pieces of recent research on adult development and mid-life in particular.

I was thirty-four when I wrote *Growing Pains in Ministry* and the above mentioned article. Roy Mooney, who had served as my Provincial a few years earlier, asked me at the time whether any of what I wrote would be of help to me when I reached mid-life myself. In retrospect it has; I know now, however, that I lacked experience when I ambitiously put pen to paper to write that book and article. Hence, what appears here is a fresh approach to an old and favorite topic. Also, while written from the perspective of a North American, the book does include some examples that I hope apply generally to people from countries and cultures other than my own.

No book comes to life without the help of others. The present one is no exception to that rule. A number of people read parts of it while it was in the making and offered many helpful criticisms. A word of thanks to: Jane Amirault, RGS, Renato Cruz, FMS, Michael de Waas, FMS, Fernand Dostie, FMS, Craig Evans, ACSW, Roland Faley, TOR, Virginia Fornasa, SMSM, Thomas Giardino, SM, Teodoro Grageda, FMS, John Harhager, SM, Paul Hennessy, CFC, Ken Hogan, FMS, Charles Howard, FMS, Kathleen Kelley, Ph.D., John E. Kerrigan, Jr., Chanel Leonard, FMS, Marie Kraus, SND, John Malich, FMS, John McDonnell, FMS, Rea McDonnell, SSND, Patrick McNamara, FMS, Roy Mooney, FMS, John P. Nash, FMS, John Perring-Mulligan, PhD, Peggy Perring-Mulligan, MA, Raymond Pasi, FMS, Luke Pearson, FMS, John Philips,

FMS, Jude Pieterse, FMS, Hank Sammon, FMS, Mary Sammon, Allen Sherry, FMS, Brian Sweeney, FMS, Steve Synan, FMS, Patrick Tonry, SM, and Katherine Wolff, NDS. The strengths of this book are due to their generous assistance; the author must claim credit for its weaknesses.

A word of thanks, too, to Edmund Lane, SSP, my editor at Alba House. From the outset he believed in this project and encouraged it. I am grateful for his openness, his enthusiasm, and his patient work with me in bringing this book to life.

This book is dedicated to John Perring-Mulligan, a dear friend of almost three decades. He has been a mentor to me in ways he may not realize. We have been fellow travelers on the mid-life journey; he and his wife Peggy have also been a great support to me in my vocation as a Marist Brother and during the ups-and-downs that marked the last few years. I treasure their friendship. Several months ago, Eugene Kabanguka, one of my Rwandan Marist Brothers, said to me, "You are becoming like a brother to me." I thanked him, sure in myself that I knew what he meant. But he continued, "You don't know what I mean, do you?" Now not so sure of myself and curious, I asked what he meant. Eugene responded, "Here in Africa when we say, 'You are like a brother to me,' we mean that we share the same blood." That's the way it is with John. What a blessing beyond measure for me!

A word too about Chris. Assassinated at age 43 — he left us much too soon. I miss his generous heart, his impish spirit, his many questions about life, and mid-life in particular. Most of all, though, I miss him. Something tells me that I always will. With that said, let's get started.

Sean D. Sammon, FMS
Dadiangas, the Philippines
October 24, 1995

LIFE AFTER YOUTH

CHAPTER I

MID-LIFE TUMOR

*I*ts symptoms crept in by night, like those invasion forces that come ashore in the early morning hours before dawn. Over time they made themselves at home. Strength sapped, weight gained, mood shifted. I hardly noticed. Were there good reasons for the changes? Of course. All of them rational: too much work, too much travel, the hard coin of mid-life.

A routine physical examination handed down the diagnosis. Isn't it always that way: mundane, uneventful, startling. A pituitary tumor. "It's extensive," the doctor said, "five centimeters and benign. You will need surgery." Walking in at forty-six and self-reporting good health, you leave diminished, lacking. You pass over from person to patient.

How quickly illness alters life. All those plans, tied tightly in place, become undone. A move is put off, new work postponed, life reorganized. The hardest part, though, is the endless telling of the story. How different the reactions of people. Some become ministers and console; others avoid you, wonder, "What to say?" and, speechless, wander off; still others reverse roles, making you the caretaker. It's disconcerting to be ill and managing others — but it happens.

Years ago a friend said, "The death of one of us will mark our loss of innocence." Believe me, you think about it — wondering if you are going to be the one to mark his loss of innocence. Others wonder that, too; they just do not tell you.

"You will need replacement hormones as we start to treat the tumor." Then there is the endless waiting: for medicine to work, tissue to shrink, some semblance of health to return. You see yourself differently and you need to be seen, to let others know that you are still among the living. And you start to keep secrets, too.

After all, you were sick and did not know it. Like a careful researcher you pore over comments passed along in recent years: "You look so tired"; "Why so pale?" "My, haven't we gained weight!" "You're working too hard." Was it two years ago that blood pressure began to climb? What about that high cholesterol count, the one that would not budge even when cheese and ice cream were history? "Where was I?" you wonder; "didn't I see what was happening to me?"

I missed the leave-takings too. Sexuality, that tender brother of mine, was among the first to depart. How well I remember the fear and illusion of our first meeting so long ago; how much I miss the passionate union of our middle age, so hard won these past ten years. Sister sensuality fell victim too; wet wool, crisp cotton, the tender caress of a friend — all lost their power to please.

There's also the indignation, yours and others: was an early diagnosis missed? What about the joint pain, wounds that would not heal, headaches, and umpteen other complaints of recent years? You flail about, looking for someone to blame; all the while the tumor grows, nestled under your brain, happy and at home.

You become a frequent visitor to the tomb-like MRI. Strapped in place, earphones and Vivaldi masking the incessant banging, you meet the isolation of illness. In that solitary place your demons appear. A perennially slow learner, you begin to realize that no one else can make the journey to health for you.

Where is God in all this? Surely not responsible for what has happened, but there, nevertheless, in powerful ways — present, listening when others have tired of all the details, a consolation when you wake in the dead of night. There's no magic to God. That realization helps you understand the purpose of sickness. It forces you to be yourself. You lose that public face of yours and find the one that God sees.

The loss of health is a great equalizer; it's the continual shedding of clothes that eventually peels down to the person that you thought you were.

Finally, the surgery comes. How like a journey to another country: the tight embraces, faces tender and frightened at the same time, the reassurances. Departing from this touch of humanity, you are wheeled into a stainless steel and sterile world. Banks of TV monitors, harsh ceiling lights, a narrow table, and the cold. Always the cold, you cannot shake it. You wonder: how close will your time here bring you to the other side?

The team arrives. Masked, they struggle to make contact. "I love this surgery," says one; "Good morning," another; still another, "My name is Kay." Somehow healing will take a giant step in this place, among strangers.

Hours later I struggle with a dreamlike waking from anesthesia. My first thought, "What time is it?" The second, "Where am I?" The reassuring hand of a nurse connects me with the world I left for a while. It is good to be home.

Illness leaves you between lives, the one you knew and another that awaits you. Then, you were in control, enjoyed the upper hand; now, the future is less certain, beyond your power to shape. You learn the importance of patience.

"So what have you learned?" people ask. That is just the

point — mid-life illness does not teach you anything. Instead, it helps you understand, for the first time. And you know full well that that understanding will someday answer to the name of wisdom.

CHAPTER II

LIFE AFTER YOUTH

*M*id-life illness helped me to understand the wisdom of five simple points.

One: *Take time to befriend your real self.* Former Iran hostage Morehead Kennedy was right: "When you've been through a life-threatening experience, you are confronted suddenly with your real self." Kennedy also passed along this piece of sage advice, "Don't chase after an idealized self. Come to terms instead with the person that you are in fact."

Two: *Realize that more years in life have come and gone than lie ahead.* By mid-life I had to admit that I had probably lived already more years than the number that remained for me. Denial, though, died hard. With surgery behind me, for example, feelings of invincibility crept in again. What returned me to my senses? The comments of a doctor in Rome. "So you had a brain tumor!" she said. My response? "I prefer to think of it as a pituitary tumor." "I know," she said, "but it was a brain tumor. Furthermore, another year of life for that tumor would have cost you your own." What a difference that realization made.

Three: *Be a mentor: help others clear up some of the questions they have about life!* As we grow older many of us realize that it's important to give something back to life. Mentoring the next generation is one good way to do just that. At forty-seven the urgency grew stronger in me to look out for those who came after me. Not as a parent, but like an older brother. No longer longing for children of my own, it became my way to pass along life.

Four: *Stop remaking God over into your own image and likeness.* At mid-life I gave up the God of life's first half to be open to the embrace of the God of life's afternoon. How? By moving away from the experimental quality of early adulthood and towards the inward focus of the middle years. Several people reminded me to conclude my mid-life journey by coming home to myself; when I arrived finally at the place where I belonged, I found that God was among those waiting to receive me.

Five: *Accept the fact that self-transcendence and not self-fulfillment is the goal of human and spiritual growth.* By mid-life I realized more fully than before that fundamental to my human and spiritual growth and that of others was the awareness of our communion with one another.

Each lesson mentioned above has its origin in a developmental task of mid-life: *Reworking identity, facing mortality, becoming a mentor, discovering God — often for the very first time, transcending yourself.* How do we address each of them? In part, by evaluating past life decisions and accomplishments as well as the direction and meaning of the previous four or so decades of our life. In so doing, we reexamine early dreams and values in our attempt to understand just how these ideals had been lived out or omitted from our life. Oscar Wilde used a bit of irony to describe this last task. "The gods have two ways of dealing harshly with us," he said, "the first is to deny us our dreams, and the second is to grant them."

This chapter lays the groundwork for our discussion of mid-life. Demographers report that during the 1990's approxi-

mately 12,000 people in the U.S. will turn forty each day.[1]
Should their projection be true, more than a few of us will be
looking for an adequate answer to this question: "Is there life
after youth?" Let's start to develop a response to it by describing the transition into mid-life and its common characteristics.

MID-LIFE TRANSITION DESCRIBED

Antonio Gramsci said it well when he wrote in his *Prison Notebooks*: "The crisis consists precisely in the fact that the old is
dying and the new cannot yet be born; in this interregnum a
great variety of morbid symptoms appear."[2] The four-to-five
year period of life evaluation and change, called *mid-life transition*, begins for most of us somewhere in the late thirties to
early forties. Today, however, we realize also that, for those who
delayed earlier life commitments — marriage, parenthood, entrance into seminary — the transition at mid-life may not get
underway until almost age fifty.

The predictable crisis times in adult development, then,
no longer appear quite so predictable. From the beginning of
this century until the mid-1970's, for example, the marker
events of life — graduation, first job, marriage, first child, empty
nest, retirement, widowhood, even death — tended to occur
for most of us at predictable times in life.[3]

The same pattern held true for those of us who are priests
and men and women religious. Age for ordination and first and
final vows was fairly well determined. After all, just forty years
ago if we entered seminary or religious life during our twenties
we were considered "late vocations"!

In contrast, while we leave childhood sooner today, we
are taking longer to grow up and much longer to die. For example, a woman in the U.S. who reaches her fiftieth birthday

today, and remains free of cancer and heart disease, can expect to celebrate her ninety-second year.[4]

For some of us, then, adulthood may not get underway until age thirty; for others, age fifty is what forty used to be. In the face of these facts, anyone of us might ask: how can I know that the mid-life transition has begun to unfold in my life? Time starts to pinch: yes, by mid-life we begin to realize that the real currency of life is time, not money!

For many of us some crisis in our forties or early fifties forces us to examine what we are going to do with the second half of life. This question begins to loom large: "How shall I live the rest of my life?" Behind it lies a spiritual query: *"On whom or what do I set my heart?"* Regardless of our age at onset, however, it is important to remember this fact: at the outset of the mid-life transition early adulthood is dying but the era of middle adulthood has not yet come to life. The period between these two events, the transition at mid-life, is important in the life of each of us for several reasons.

Mid-life Tasks

Do you think much about death these days? More often, say, than ten years ago? Most of us face the question of personal mortality for the first time about age forty. We start to realize that death, along with happening to everyone else, will also pay a visit to us. We should not be surprised at this development. After all, accepting our mortality is at the core of the transition at mid-life.

Many young adults identify easily with this quip of the late novelist William Saroyan, "Everybody has got to die, but I believe an exception will be made in my case!" Those of us in mid-life, in contrast, are compelled to face the fact that we have joined the ranks of those for whom death will eventually be a personal experience. Three developments conspire to convince us of this reality: (a) the death or increasing dependence of parents, older relatives, colleagues, and friends, (b) the unexpected death of contemporaries — is the obituary column an early stop for you on your journey through the daily newspaper? — and (c) our own physical decline.

The transition at mid-life also serves as a bridge between early and middle adulthood. In moving from one era to the next, we become aware of the gap that exists between what we once dreamed of becoming and what we have in fact become. The mid-life transition can include feelings of depression and emptiness; we are also faced with the task of mourning opportunities missed, decisions made or avoided, and experiences pursued or denied. Those parts of us that were neglected or inhibited during earlier years clamor now for attention.

Obviously, then, mid-life can be painful. It can, however, also provide us with a newfound freedom, leaving us less eager to please others and no longer counting on their evaluation of our performance for our sense of self-esteem. Mid-life does not necessarily mean decline; many of us eventually count these years as among those of greatest well-being in our lives. Coping with the upheaval of mid-life transition can also be made somewhat easier if we accept the fact that the conventional wisdom, which states that stability should mark the adult years, is simply not true.

MID-LIFE'S PLACE IN THE LIFECYCLE

Nature tells us a great deal about the lifecycle of adults. Over the years the life of each of us evolves through seasons or stages similar to those found in nature. There are new beginnings filled with a sense of springtime excitement, and separations and leave-takings marked by pain and a sense of autumnal death. Feelings of well-being are associated with the summertime of life, while bleakness and despair can take on the character of a personal New England winter.

Where does mid-life fit into the cycle of life? Between early and late adulthood. For the purposes of our discussion, the years of our adult life can be divided into early, middle, late, and late-late adulthood. As one of these eras is winding down, another is already getting under way. Early adulthood encompasses the period from our late teen years until mid-life at about age forty. For many of us, it is life's most stressful time. Beginning with mid-life and continuing to about age sixty-five, we experience middle adulthood — often our most productive and, in retrospect, satisfying time in life. Late adulthood follows until late, late adulthood gets underway about age eighty. During these two latter eras we build upon the developmental work of earlier years. It is important to remember, too, that each era has its distinguishing characteristic features.

We are moved from era to era by the fundamental changing character of our lives. For example, a man in his early forties may notice that he is reassessing the direction and meaning of his involvements, relationships, and commitments. His life's character will be influenced importantly by his growing awareness that at present he has probably lived more years than the number that lie ahead for him. Over the course of a few years, this man will begin to make changes as he moves from early to middle adulthood.

Forces and Circumstances Shaping our Life Structure

Various forces and circumstances also shape the structure of our lives. For example, particular historical events and contemporary conditions work together to shape our understanding of our world, ourselves, and other people. Those of us who grew up during the Great Depression, the Vietnam War, or the post-Vatican II renewal realize how significant these events were in shaping our attitudes towards money, authority, and religious belief.

Four out of every ten Americans today, for example, belong to the Vietnam generation (born 1946-1955).[5] Highly individualistic, many of them delayed making life commitments, and, unlike their predecessors, questioned authority and challenged American institutions and corporate paternalism. A significant number, however, also appeared more inner-directed and adventuresome spiritually.

The members of this generation, now in mid-life, identify 1968 as their watershed year. The war in Vietnam, a universal draft, the assassinations of Martin Luther King and Robert Kennedy, the Democratic convention in Chicago that summer: all these events worked together to shape their consciousness.

What characteristic most distinguishes the members of this generation from those that came before? They have done some things very differently than their predecessors! A 1989 *Fortune* magazine article, for example, reported that men and women of the Vietnam generation have called into question the role of leadership: apparently "they don't like telling others what to do anymore than they like being told."[6]

We are affected, too, by our socio-cultural world, ethnic group, race, socio-economic class, religion, and political system. The various roles we carry out also shape our lives. We may be parents, husbands, wives, friends, single persons, sisters, priests, or brothers, lovers, separated or divorced persons, bosses or members of any one of a dozen different groups and organizations. Each circumstance helps shape the structure of our life; each role we assume during our lifetime helps us live out one or more parts of ourselves.

In contrast, these roles and influences also inhibit the development of our personality. In choosing to live out particular roles, we must necessarily neglect other aspects of ourselves. Keep this important point in mind: no one life structure, that is, our way of being in the world with all that entails — occupation, relationships, vocational choices, religious practices, etc. — will allow us to live out all our various dreams, values, and potential roles and personality characteristics. As a result, we need to modify or change our life structure from time to time to allow some of the neglected, inhibited parts of ourselves to be expressed. Periods of life transition provide us the means to do just that.

Before saying more about these important times of change, though, let's take a moment to explain further the term *life structure*. Psychologist Daniel Levinson encourages us to focus on the choices we make in life and how we deal with their consequences when describing the concept.[7] What important choices do we make during the adult years? Those having to do with family, friendships and love relationships of various types, work, leisure, religious belief, political persuasion, place of residence, and immediate and long-term goals.

Levinson points out that the components of any life structure are not a random set of items, like pebbles washed up on the shore. Instead, like the threads of a tapestry, they are woven into a particular design. Some components in our life structure hold more importance than others. In general, one or two occupy a central place while others are more peripheral. Still others are quite marginal. Those components that are central, of course, receive the largest share of our time and energy and influence strongly the other choices we make in life.

A young married man, for example, may spend his twenties and thirties concentrating on developing a career. Over time his job and all that it entails become the center of his life. As a consequence, his relationships with his wife and family suffer from time to time. About mid-life, though, this same man may find that his focus begins to shift, with family and other relationships in his life taking on more importance. Over the period of several years he will have to make choices that alter his life structure so as to allow him to incorporate this change in focus into his day-to-day living.

PERIODS OF STABILITY AND TRANSITION

Our life structure does not change suddenly or capriciously, nor does it remain static. Rather, it evolves through a series of alternating stable and transitional periods, lasting in general six to seven and four to five years each, respectively. Five years on the average for a transitional period to run its course! Does that mean that you and I will awake every morning, day in and day out, to face questions like: "Where am I going in life?" Not really. During a time of transition, the vast majority of us continue to function *externally* in much the same way as we always have. *Internally*, however, we know that our self-understanding and outlook on others, God, and life is undergoing considerable change.

What is a stable period? Although some change does occur during these years, in general our basic life structure remains constant during a stable period. It has three critical phases during which we (1) make certain important choices about our lives,

(2) begin to build a life structure around these choices, and (3) work to attain particular goals and values within this structure.

In contrast, during a period of transition we terminate our existing life structure and work toward initiating a new one within which to live during the ensuing stable period. Journalist Gail Sheehy uses the image of a lobster shedding its series of hard, protective shells to describe the phenomenon.[8] Each time this crustacean expands from within, it must slough off its confining shell. Until a new covering grows, it is left unprotected and vulnerable but also yeasty and embryonic once again. The same description can be applied to each of us during any time of life transition.

Marked by an impulse toward change, these periods of growth are critical in the process of self-renewal: they help us to re-invent ourselves time and again. Levinson refers to them as times for second thoughts.[9] Transitional periods also share these three characteristics: (1) an ending, followed by (2) a seemingly unproductive "time-out" during which we feel disconnected from other people and things in the past and emotionally unconnected to the present — "lost at sea" — and finally (3) a new beginning. To benefit from a transition, we must make a reappraisal as to what has happened in our life, explore possibilities for change in ourselves and our world, and eventually move toward making certain choices that will form the basis for our new life structure.

Transitional periods, then, are marked by a feeling of being "up in the air," which is endurable if it is part of a movement toward a desired end. For many of us, however, it appears unrelated to any larger or beneficial pattern and hence is quite distressing.

TRANSITIONS BEGIN WITH AN ENDING

As mentioned earlier, every transition begins with an ending. Some of us, for example, will report feelings of stagnation or of being stuck in a rut. For others, the transition starts with a change in circumstances such as the death of a loved one, an outstanding personal achievement, a setback or outright failure, or a new job or relationship.

Still others of us — by the decisions we make — "choose" to get a transition underway. We place ourselves in new circumstances, cut ties with our old world, question the very foundation upon which we have based our life to date. Those of us who are members of this last group, aware of the upheaval and pain that will ensue as a result of our actions, realize too that more troubling consequences will be our lot if we "play it safe" at this time in our life.

Even transitional situations that appear to be new beginnings include the ambivalent experience of letting go. After all, to make a move to a new and personally challenging job, we must move away from our present work and all that it entails. The process of mourning is, for most of us, an important part of any transition's first phase. As with any other experience of grief, we often experience anger and sadness along with feelings of relief and wonder. Perhaps the simplest way to identify the beginning of a transition in your own life is to ask yourself this question: "If I were to write an autobiography, when would I pen this phrase: A chapter of my life came to a close when…?"

Our particular style of dealing with termination will influence our approach to any life transition. Quite honestly, though, whether initiated by ourselves or someone else, most of us handle endings poorly. Two examples, representing the extremes, illustrate this point. On the one hand, you or I may be a person who dashes away from any ending, leaving a job for the last time a day ahead of schedule to avoid any awkward or painful good-byes. Or, on the other hand, we might be the type of person who lingers in the face of any possible ending, reluctant to let go of parts of ourselves, an experience, or a situation.

Some priests, sisters, and brothers, for example, never seem to get around to moving all their personal belongings from one community to another when they are reassigned. This failure to make a break with the past gives them an excuse to return time and again to their former home. Those who lived with them the previous year begin to wonder: "Has this person, in fact, moved to a new community or is he or she still living with us?" Whether our style of ending is abrupt and change-denying or slow and gradual or somewhere in between, it will influence our approach to any life change.

The first step of any transition, then, includes the feeling of "falling apart." We feel some loss and emptiness; some wonder whether they are betraying their past. To arrive somewhere new, however, we have first to leave somewhere else.

TRANSITIONS END WITH A NEW BEGINNING

Every transition also ends with a beginning. We enter a period of stability and feel as though a new chapter of our life has opened up. How can we be sure that a new beginning is underway? When we can report that our attention is more and more focused on the future and that we are less occupied with the task of reevaluating the past.

English novelist John Galsworthy, however, warned us not to think of new beginnings as necessarily neat and orderly; he wrote, "The beginnings of all human undertakings are untidy."[10] New beginnings can be indirect and unimpressive: they start inside us and depend upon an inner realignment of deep longings, values, and motivations. Think again about writing that autobiography; when would you jot down these words: "A new chapter of my life got underway when…"?

We cannot force a new beginning; when we are ready to make one, we will do so. With that said, however, we also need to keep these two guidelines in mind. First of all, when the time is right for change, we need to stop getting ready to act, and act. Preparing for a new chapter in life becomes for some of us an endless task. Just as therapy clients can spend their time collecting insights but avoiding behavioral change, some of us keep putting off making a new beginning. When the time is right — just "do it"!

Second, we need to think of ourselves as progressing toward our goal. Whether we are moving from one city to another, ending a relationship, or providing more leisure time in a busy schedule, let's avoid getting preoccupied with immediate results. Concentrate, instead, on moving toward our goal, not on the goal itself. Remember: life transitions take time, four to five years on the average; we don't have to be sprinters dashing away from the starting line.

AN IMPORTANT FALLOW TIME
LIES AT THE HEART OF EVERY TRANSITION

Between the times of ending and new beginning, however, lies an important fallow period, a Sabbath time, which is at the heart of all transitions and the mid-life transition in particular. During it we examine our values, goals, and aspirations and question whether our present life structure is fostering or hindering their realization.

This middle phase of a transition is an extremely important one. One man compared the discomfort accompanying it to stopping in the middle of a busy thoroughfare in order to think. "Once you step off the curb," he said, "you need to get quickly to the other side. You'd have to be crazy to sit down in the middle of the street and figure things out."[11] Crazy or not, the transition's middle phase calls for us to stop and take stock. We are often surprised, and sometimes awed, by what we find!

Familiar problem-solving techniques, for example, generally don't work so well as in the past. We often suffer from increased stress and are filled with doubts. Some find so little meaning in their lives that they question the purpose of living. Leo Tolstoy gives this powerful description of the middle phase of one of his life's transitions: "I felt that something had broken within me on which my life had always rested, that I had nothing to hold on to, and that morally my life had stopped."[12]

Times of transition are more turbulent for some of us than for others. Consider the following dramatic example. It illustrates the type of upheaval that is the lot of many during the fallow period that makes up any life transition's core. Imagine that you suffer the misfortune of spending the month of August in Washington, D.C. or Rome, Italy. The phrase "hazy, hot, and humid" doesn't half describe weather conditions in both these cities at that time of the year.

Seeking some relief from the heat, you escape the city for a few days and check into a hotel in a resort area situated on a large lake. One afternoon, while lying on the beach, you spy a boat moored to a dock on the other side of the lake and decide to swim across and check it out. As you get ready to jump into the lake, however, you notice something else, also very common on hazy, hot, and humid afternoons in August: thunder clouds. But you tell yourself: "I'm a strong swimmer, those clouds are a long way off, I'll be over and back before the storm moves in." So, you dive in and start to swim; when you are half way across the lake your luck runs out. Those clouds were traveling a bit faster than you estimated. Consequently, you are now in the middle of the lake in a thunder and lightning storm.

Let's suppose that you have the presence of mind to say, "I've got two options: I can swim back to the shore I just left and I'll be safe or I can head toward the boat and I'll be OK." As you look for that shore you just quit, however, you cannot find it; due to the storm, it is shrouded now in fog. And that boat toward which you were swimming in the first place? In the violence of the storm it has broken free of its moorings and drifted to the far end of the lake. There you are, in the middle of a lake — in the midst of a thunder and lightning storm — with "zero" options. For some of us, that's what it feels like to be in the midst of a life transition.

You might protest, "Don't I have a lot of company there in the middle of the lake?" Yes, you do; perhaps we can all drown together. This illustration reminds us that during any time of life transition, about all we can be sure of is this simple truth: *"We cannot go back to where we came from, but we're not really sure where we are going."*

Experience indicates that all of us must surrender to the emptiness of these times of change and not struggle to escape them. The middle phase of any transition offers the possibility of transformation. A full understanding of life transitions is a necessary part not only of the cycle of dying and rising but also of Christian belief. The death to life experience — the fact that we must die to be born anew — is central to nature, to Christianity, and to everyone's life. The Lenten season in the Christian churches, for example, is a fallow in-between time during which believers are encouraged to reflect seriously on Jesus' life and their own spiritual journey. For some of us, fasting and penance mark the season. For all of us, it ends with the glorious new beginning of the Resurrection and the Easter season.

TRANSITIONS TAKE YEARS

Two important points should be noted in our discussion of transitional periods. In the first place, every transition lasts for an average of four to five years. The changes that occur during these periods are not overnight events. They evolve over many months, even years.

Second, during any transition we need to explore new ways of being in the world. Then the choices which we make to initiate a new life structure are not the end product of an isolated intellectual exercise. John Coleman, former president of Haverford College, took up this challenge during a two-month sabbatical. He worked as a garbage collector, ditch digger, and sandwich man in a Boston restaurant.

On his return to the university, many among his surprised faculty raised some pointed questions about his sanity. To those Haverford students with questions about the direction they wanted their lives to take and whether a college education had a place in that journey, however, Coleman had always given this advice: "Experience something very different from that with which you are familiar; put yourself into life circumstances that will throw your everyday life into sharp relief. In this way, you will be better able to make serious life decisions." Coleman took his own advice and was pleased with both the experience and the results. He later utilized the knowledge gained during his sabbatical when he became president of a foundation: he reshaped its field of activities so that its projects included the lives of blue collar workers.

Transitional periods, then, take time, necessitate exploring new ways of being in the world, and call forth our personal style of dealing with endings in life.

Regardless of individual differences, these times of reevaluation and change have an impact on our relationships, commitments, work, and understanding of our personality and world.

They also affect those with whom we share our life. In Chapter IV we will meet Eddie Anderson, a fictional character in Elia Kazan's novel *The Arrangement.* Anderson's family thought that he had lost his mind when he embarked on his mid-life transition. Has your experience been similar? Family and colleagues, or the members of your diocese or religious institute, reacting strongly to what they see happening to you?

Some will advise us to ignore the very important questions raised by the experience of transition; their advice: stop all this introspection and get on with life. Others, judging growth observed during the adult years as erratic and unpredictable, will saddle us with the label *middlescent*, an adolescent the second time around. Still others, unwilling to embrace the transitions in their own lives, deny that anything of significance is taking place in ours. They have a vested interest in maintaining the status quo: to convince themselves that transitions don't occur for us helps them maintain the myth that they surely don't happen in their lives.

Thankfully, there are a number of people who will applaud the courage we demonstrate in talking about developmental changes during our middle years. They will also reassure us that greater understanding about life transitions, and their structure and length of duration, will help all of us realize that these times of upheaval and change are normal, indeed necessary, parts of what it means to be an adult.

During a transition, then, we learn that our previous life structure is now inadequate. As a result, career, ministry, marriage, relationships of various sorts, and major life commitments must be reexamined. The feelings of disengagement, disenchantment, and disorganization that accompany any life transition are common. Painful as they may seem, these periods are essential because they assist us in moving from one era of the lifecycle to the next. At mid-life, the transition we experience is an essential bridge between the stress and turmoil of early adulthood and the journey inward that so clearly marks the middle years.

Reflection Questions

Take a few minutes alone and consider the following questions. You might want to jot down a few of your thoughts for later reflection and possible discussion with others.

1. How are you different today from who you were ten years ago? What are the rewards of this current period in your life? What challenges and disappointments do you face during this time in your life?

2. Identify a time of transition in your life and consider the following questions.

   a. Can you identify its characteristic shape: an ending, followed by a fallow time and, eventually, a new beginning?

   b. Describe each stage of this transition and your feelings as you moved through it.

   c. What changes did the transition bring about in your life?

NOTES

[1] Gail Sheehy, *New Passages: Mapping Your Life Across Time* (New York: Random House, 1995), p. 58.

[2] Antonio Gramsci, *Selections from the Prison Notebooks of Antonio Gramsci*, Quintin Hoare and Geoffrey Nowell Smith, trans. and ed. (London: Lawrence & Wishart, 1971), p. 276.

[3] Sheehy, *New Passages*, p. 3.

[4] Comment made by Dr. Kenneth Manton, demographer at Duke University, Spring 1993. Cited in Sheehy, *New Passages*, p. 5.

[5] Sheehy, *New Passages*, pp. 33-37.

[6] Walter Kiechel III, "The Workaholic Generation," *Fortune*, April 10, 1989.

[7] Daniel Levinson et al., *The Seasons of a Man's Life* (New York, NY: Alfred A. Knopf, 1978), pp. 43-44.

[8] Sheehy, *New Passages*, p. 12.

[9] Levinson, *Seasons*, p. 84.

[10] John Galsworthy, *Over the River* (London: William Heineman, 1933), p. 4.

[11] William Bridges, *Transitions* (Reading, MA: Addison-Wesley, 1980), pp. 112-113.

[12] This quotation and an extended account of Tolstoy's crisis appear in his autobiographical work, *A Confession*, trans. Aylmer Maude (London: Oxford University Press, 1940).

CHAPTER III

MID-LIFE MORTALITIES

*M*id-life mortalities — those little deaths that start to creep in about age forty — have been constant companions of late. So many months, among the past dozen, bear the trace of one or another. It started with my brain tumor. Have twelve months and more passed since a routine blood examination gave rise to that troubling diagnosis? A year has come and gone since surgeons removed the tumor: a lonely and frightening swim through a sea of cold steel, harsh lights, and the healing hands of strangers.

Twelve months, too, since I felt the shame. Yes, sickness shamed me: in the eyes of others and, unfortunately, too often in my own, I was damaged goods. Examined thoroughly, I was found wanting. I joined an invisible community of the sick. We have our ways of recognizing one another and a language uniquely our own. It resists translation, its vocabulary recorded in the dictionary of uncertainty and human suffering.

I am well now. Doctors confirm that fact; so too does that more reliable inner physician we all possess. In the eyes of many others, though, I shall never be well again. That's right, never well again. In every conversation people eventually ask the question: "What about your health?" Puffed up by the illusion that my post-operative recovery is obvious, I am quickly deflated like a balloon whose robust life is threatened by a steady escape of air.

One day, weeks after the surgery, the doctor said, "Another year of life for this tumor would have cost you your own." How quickly illness divides a generation into those who understand and those who think they do. Mid-life sickness brings you face to face with yourself. No longer, for example, can I deny this startling fact: more years have come and gone than lie ahead. Yes, more years have come and gone than lie ahead.

My illness, even with its cure, was but one harbinger of mortality among twelve unrelenting months of them. Another was the death of my friend and fellow Marist Brother Chris Mannion. By forty haven't most of us surrendered any hope of making friends like those of life's first half? Fellow travelers who knew us when and, though they could have chosen otherwise, loved us enough to make the journey alongside. At forty-six I found that mid-life friendship with Chris captured youth's freshness in the seasoned wood of middle age.

"I'm growing fond of you," he said one day. This friendship grew like so many others, a step at a time. One day a word, a tender touch the next, eventually, secrets shared. Isn't friendship always like that: a fragile flower slowly finding its way to life. Death stole away this brother of mine. Was it but a year ago the search began: for an explanation; for some sense in the face of senselessness; eventually, for what was left of him.

How precious life becomes when death snatches it away. A Rwandan soldier's bullet brought that news: quick, efficient, shocking, deadly. Killing Chris, it continued its journey, traveling through me and so many others, tearing open the interconnected webs of our lives. Its handiwork cannot be undone; the passage of time fails to tailor the broken threads left in its wake.

"He was in the wrong place at the wrong time — an unintended victim of this war," a soldier later lied. The wrong place at the wrong time: a rather euphemistic way of describing a soldier's bullet to the head.

At mid-life there is a lot of dying to be done. Illusions are among the casualties. Mine died hard. Those bothersome illusions about others, this world of ours, and illusions about ourselves. These last are the most difficult to put to rest. How like consigning a loved one to the earth.

Mortalities at mid-life stole away my innocence and helped me understand that I was no longer young. Never again would I experience the world in quite the same way. I'm embarrassed to say that now I notice the flowers, and see their color and shape as if for the very first time. I take time to nap in the sun too, even on the coldest of days — content as a cat perched on a window sill to let its warmth and brilliance nourish my soul. Each morning I welcome serenades from the competing choirs of birds that line the vestry of my garden.

Mid-life mortalities also cooled my love affair with work. No longer do I steal away to spend one hour after another with this jealous partner and her endless and demanding tasks. How I resent it when others try to coax me back into line with their bad example or empty assurances about my indispensability. Time and again in recent months I've had to ask myself this question: "What fool on his deathbed ever wished there had been more time to labor?"

Mid-life mortalities set me on a journey homeward towards myself: sensually, and spiritually too. For me God had to perish in the process, or at least the God I knew. I had spent a lifetime trying to make over this God of ours, to fashion in my image and likeness rather than accept that it is the other way round. My poor language and paltry images failed eventually, leaving me to face this solitary question: "Could I let God love me as God chose to — in God's way, not mine?" Make no mistake about it: this God of ours has a passion for us. That fact helps me and maybe all mid-life lovers understand passion, once again, as if for the very first time.

Mid-life and its deaths, large and small, introduced me, in the end, to a side of myself that early in life I took pains to avoid. That cauldron of darkness that bubbles inside each of us has begun in me to see the light of day. Some call it their shadow; for me — well, it was all that I did not want to know about myself. Here at mid-life the person I thought I was and the one I so long avoided getting to know are finally meeting and becoming friends. I do foolish things these day; sometimes I secretly think I am crazy. "How out of character," I say. My behavior frightens but delights me, too. Really, I surprise my-self and ask: *"Where have you been all these years?"*

You know, our lives each day depend upon a series of tiny miracles. As we grow older we begin to understand that fact and also the wisdom of this paradox: the very things in life that we think might end it, end up making that life worth living. At forty-seven I am blessed with the hope that mortalities at mid-life might just be for me a surprising source of new life.

CHAPTER IV

THE TRANSITION AT MID-LIFE

*W*riting about his deceased friend Hugh Pierce, author Tobias Wolff had this to say, "Instead of remembering Hugh as I knew him, I too often think of him in terms of what he never had a chance to be. The things the rest of us know, he will not know. He will not know what it is to make a life with someone else. To have a child slip in beside him as he lies reading on a Sunday morning. To work at, and then look back on, a labor of years. Watch the decline of his parents, and attend to their dissolution. Lose faith. Pray anyway. Persist. We are meant to persist, to complete the whole tour. That's how we find out who we are.

"We were very close, and would have gone on being close, as I am with my other good friends from those years. He would have been one of them, another godfather for my children, another big-hearted man for them to admire and stay up late listening to. *An old friend, someone I couldn't fool, who would hold me to the best dreams of my youth as I would hold him to his.*"[13] Wolff's poignant words, we shall see as this chapter unfolds, capture well some of mid-life's challenges and rewards.

The vast majority of today's U.S. mid-lifers, however, do not feel like mid-lifers at all.[14] Having spent the last two decades dieting, exercising, and staying fit, many carry around in their heads an image of a self eight to ten years younger. In spite of this fact, some men still arrive at forty asking this traditional mid-life question: *"Is this the last chance I have to pull away from the pack?"* The competitive instinct that so marked their early years remains alive and well as this period of development gets underway. A shift in attitude must take place in them over the next few years of life — a move from competing to connecting — if they are to accomplish well the work of the transition.[15]

Those of us who are mid-life priests, sisters, and brothers in the U.S. also share the lot of our contemporaries: the experience of "eternal youth." As the median age of many religious orders increases, the definition of a young brother, priest, or sister changes accordingly. In response to my query about the age of the "young sister" being discussed during a meeting several weeks ago, for example, I was told that she was fifty-eight! A *young* sister — yes, it is all very relative.

In this chapter and Chapter VI we will examine the transition at mid-life and the years that follow. Our work in the present chapter begins with a discussion about mid-life differences: between men and women and between the approach of one person and another to the tasks of these years. Next, we take a closer look at the transition from early to middle adulthood and identify further some of its characteristic features and the questions that often accompany it. As part of this effort, we examine briefly these topics: the Dream, mid-life identity, mentoring, and the evaluation of life commitments at the onset of the middle years.

As we begin, though, keep these three points in mind. First of all, the central issue we all face at mid-life is the *loss of youth.*[16] It goes by many names — facing mortality, a last chance mentality, male menopause — and is the catalyst for much of the developmental work undertaken during middle adulthood.

Second, our *sense of brokenness* is mid-life's central faith issue. As mid-lifers aren't we more aware of the existence of individual and social sin? I know that here, at forty-seven, I feel, more than ever before, the need to be redeemed.

Third, what's the central psychological issue we face during the transition at mid-life? *The demise of the myth we have about ourselves!* Illusions die hard. At mid-life, however, to befriend our real self we must let die those myths we hold dear about ourselves, others, and the way our world works, and mourn their passing, too. Now, let's look at individual differences at mid-life.

INDIVIDUAL DIFFERENCES AT MID-LIFE

While some of us move through our developmental work at mid-life with hardly a ripple, others of us are in a mess for a while, stuck in a whirlpool that leaves us going around in circles.[17] Many of us in this latter group have come to the realization, often for the first time, that we are no longer in complete control over what is happening in our life. What we failed to realize early on, however, was that, in fact, we were never in complete control anyway.

As men and women we also differ in our approach to mid-life.[18] At the peak of the period, for example, many men feel stale, restless, and unappreciated; they long for closer intimate attachments. When their suppressed affective needs break through to the surface, they begin to realize how emotionally starved they are. They need to be careful not to blame others for their dilemma. Instead, by doing the work of the transition, they can befriend themselves and their feelings.

Health can be a problem for many men at mid-life, too. Most take better care of their cars than their bodies.[19] Married men, for example, still die, on the average, seven years earlier than their wives, many are depressed in their old age, and have a four times greater risk of suicide. Some men lack a vocabulary with which to express their feelings. As a consequence, they express those feelings inappropriately. At mid-life, if they resist changing their approach to the care of their bodies they set the stage for emotional and physical problems a few years down the line.

Mid-life is also the age when many men finally admit this great loss in their lives: the lack of a loving and respectful relationship with their fathers.[20] Revisiting their growing up years, they uncover deep pain and sadness due to the manner in which they had to separate from both parents. In U.S. society, mothers are encouraged to push their sons toward clear-cut separation.[21] Unable to express the hurt they experience in the process, men are wounded further when their fathers refuse to take on a nurturing role. A lifelong struggle ensues: whether or not to trust other men with their feelings. Their wariness with them leads to loneliness. A number of men fail to form tender and caring relationships with other men.

Women suffer in a different way.[22] Many feel choked by cultural values that dictate how they must behave — what author Anna Quindlan refers to as the "cult of the nice girl." A number of mid-life women, for example, looking back to ages 10 and 11, describe the sadness they experienced at having to surrender their freewheeling, funny, even fearless tomboy selves in order to "fit in."[23] One woman used a question and her answer to it to capture the change she experienced. "What happens to a girl's voice at this age?" she asked. Her response, "She loses it."

Over time, these women need to learn not to take responsibility for what angers or saddens or threatens others and to realize also that no one has to be perfect. By so doing they come to accept their own limitations and ultimately mortality. At mid-life a woman should at last be able to say, "I can finally be myself and stop trying to please everyone else."

For both men and women at mid-life, a commitment such as a good marriage, satisfaction in religious life or priesthood, devotion to a cause greater than oneself, is one of the best predictors of emotional and spiritual well-being. In contrast, those who delayed indefinitely any serious choices or commitments often arrive at age forty unsure of just about everything that is important in life.[24]

MOVING FROM EARLY TO MIDDLE ADULTHOOD

As mentioned in Chapter II, middle adulthood begins with the mid-life transition and continues until we reach our mid-sixties. What is our chief work during this period? Befriending our real self with all its complexity and contradictions. In general, however, most of us appear reluctant to take up this challenge; we delay moving from the era of early adulthood into the middle years for several reasons. To begin with, all change leads to loss. At mid-life we experience the loss of our youthful illusions as we rework our self-image and come to terms with our imperfections and those of others. About age forty, more than ever before, we sense the growing need to de-mythologize ourselves, other people and the world in which we live.

During our twenties and early thirties, for example, many of us hold fast to this false belief: we are invincible and larger than life. Why? So as to ambition and do what we think others expect and ask of us. The transition at mid-life gives us an opportunity to shed that illusion — a process of disenchantment — so as to face our personal poverty and limitations. Christian Brother James Zullo calls it "the crisis of limits."[25] Over time, we come to realize that some of our beliefs about ourselves, others and the way our world works are simply not true.

At mid-life the process of disenchantment has another benefit: it helps a number of us shake off the troubling feeling that we are impersonating an adult. During early adulthood, many of us feel like impostors. We convince ourselves that it is just a matter of time before others discover that we simply do not know what we are doing! What can we do, then, to assure that eventually we will assume full membership in the adult world? Bring to completion at mid-life the process of disenchantment and these three other developmental tasks: learn ways of relating to other men and women, become increasingly more confident in our life's work, and reduce our sense of vulnerability.

For all of us, however, the work of disenchantment gives rise to many feelings: disappointment, grief, sadness, anger, depression, but also wonder and a sense of liberation. The experience is similar to losing a family member or friend to death. The mourning takes time. Just as my relationship with a loved one is changed but not ended by death, the relationship with myself does not end at mid-life; rather it is transformed through the process of disenchantment.

Secondly, in crossing the bridge between early and middle adulthood, we lose our sense of easy immortality and begin to experience a number of "little deaths." By age forty we are also much more aware of what we've left out of life. We wonder: "Does sufficient time remain to squeeze it all in?" Many of us fear that our future will not be so good as our past.

As mentioned above, mid-life represents the beginning of the death of youth. Since most of us have had, to date, little experience with facing personal mortality, it can appear imminent. Some of us begin to feel it in the marrow of our bones. There is, for example, no longer a generation standing as a buffer between death and us. Instead, at mid-life we become aware that we are now part of the dominant generation in society, looked to as a buffer against death by younger persons.

The death of a contemporary is still eulogized as a tragedy, but now serves as an acute reminder of our own possible death through an accident or illness. Editor Howell Raines put it bluntly in his book, *Fly Fishing Through the Mid-life Crisis*: "It [is] hardly worth going to the trouble of having a mid-life crisis equal to the name if you [are] not going to figure out how to be comfortable in the embrace of what Mr. Hemingway called 'that old whore death'."[26]

Even though the physical changes that we experience at mid-life may be measurably insignificant, every graying or thinning hair, for many of us, is another reminder of age and ultimately of mortality. In another example, when the leg muscles of an eighteen-year-old boy fire, he takes off like an antelope; when a man of forty-five tries to do the same, he tears his Achilles tendon.[27]

The physical changes that many mid-life men experience bear mention.[28] A number notice a gradual decrease in muscle mass and strength while fat appears to increase. Hormonal changes can give rise to a number of symptoms ranging from broken sleep, irritability, lethargy, memory lapses, depression, and mood swings. Some men experience numbness and tingling, headaches, dizzy spells and night sweats — all associated with circulatory changes. Finally, while the high point of a man's sexual life-cycle is in his forties, as he moves into his fifties he may have intermittent difficulties gaining and sustaining erections and a lessening of sexual desire.

What about women and mid-life physical change? Some resist accepting the fact that mid-life marks their entrance into a long passage leading out of youth and fertility and into unfamiliar territory. In a society that places a high value on appearance, for example, the experience of not *looking* young rather than any sense of not *being* young can give rise to a false perception of rapid aging. One mid-life woman put it this way, "Not many forty-something women would mind being Jane Fonda's age if they could also have her physique."

While the mood swings characteristic of *peri-menopause*, however, may bring on sadness, malaise, mild depression, irritability, and poor concentration, the results of recent studies demonstrate that *post-menopausal* women, when compared to younger women, show less evidence of any psychological problems.[29] The best reward for making a conscious, disciplined trip through menopause? *Post-menopausal zest* — that special buoyant sort of energy, fueled in part by the change in ratio of testosterone to estrogen.[30]

For all of us in mid-life, our growing awareness of death causes us to reorder our time perspective. We start to view life in terms of the time we have left. Moses Herzog, a fictional character of Saul Bellow, put it this way: "Maybe I am going through a change in outlook." In recalling his mother's death, he realized that he was "one of the mature generation now, and life was his to do something with, if he could." When we begin to realize that we have lived already more years than the number that lie ahead for us, we reach an important crossroads. That small bit of knowledge makes this critical difference: most of us decide that we are no longer willing to live according to the standards and values of someone else.

Mid-life Questions

Near the end of our thirties and into our early forties, then, we once again feel the need to evaluate our lives. For those of us who spent our early adulthood becoming somebody rather than doing something we love, our victory will now seem hollow.

We begin to ask ourselves: "What have I done with my life? What have I done with myself? What are my best talents and how am I using or wasting them? What do I truly want for myself and for others? What do I truly give to and get from others? Whom do I care about; does anyone really care about me? Is it possible for me to live in a way that best combines my talents, current desires, values, and aspirations?" This spiritual question, cited also in Chapter II, is once again behind these queries: *"On whom or what do I set my heart?"*

The forties offer us the possibility of a new beginning, beyond the narrow rules and roles of life's first half.[31] We can trade in our false self and stop being ruled by the need to prove ourselves. To navigate this transition successfully, however, we must question virtually every aspect of our life. Some of us discover that the answers we find can be very unsettling indeed.

MID-LIFE CHALLENGES:

*Re-working the Dream, Re-formulating Identity,
Multi-Generational Mentoring, Re-fashioning Commitments*

1. Re-working the Dream

Mid-life offers each of us an opportunity to re-work our Dream or to fashion a new one should that be necessary. What is a life Dream? My answer to this question: *"What shall I do with my adult life?"* Emerging first during the adolescent years, the Dream serves as a guiding vision or myth. It has the potential to keep us forever honest about the direction and purpose of our life. Stated simply, we can always refer to this touchstone to judge whether or not our life choices are in keeping with our deepest beliefs and values.

Initially, the Dream is neither well-formed nor carefully

worked out. Where one exists, however, it must play an important role in the decisions we make if personal growth is to continue. After all, our Dream contains the spark that ignites a passion for life within us.

Some of us attempt to fashion a way of living out our Dream during our twenties. At about age thirty we have an opportunity to evaluate our efforts and make changes and modifications in our life structure to bring it more into line with the spirit of our Dream.

Others of us, however, betray our Dream early on: we create a life structure that chokes any possibility of it taking root and flourishing. Still others of us build a life structure that permits us to live out only part of our Dream. By age thirty, those of us in these two latter groups feel stifled. The decisions we must make will not be easy, and some losses may be entailed as we work on these two complementary tasks: moving our life more into line with our Dream while reshaping the latter to escape some of its adolescent tyranny. Work on these tasks we must, however, if emotional and spiritual growth is to continue.

The transition at mid-life provides another opportunity for work on the Dream. By age forty many of us are asking these important questions: What have I done with my early Dream? What do I want to do with it now? Do I need to change it or find a new one entirely? Eddie Anderson, a character in Elia Kazan's novel, *The Arrangement*,[32] is a case in point. This mid-life man lost all touch with his Greek heritage to the point of changing his name from Evangelah to Edwin and eventually to Eddie to satisfy the tempo and lifestyle of the California advertising firm in which he was an executive.[33] More important, in the process Eddie also betrayed his Dream of becoming a writer. He married a woman who fit in with this betrayal, and developed friends and a life pattern that almost choked his Dream to death.

The tale of Eddie Anderson begins just after he has almost killed himself in a car accident. He is unsure that it was actually an accident. As Eddie's story unfolds, we find example after example of his betrayal of his Dream. Although genitally intimate with a number of women, he is emotionally intimate with no one. His writing talents have been twisted into writing glib advertising copy, and notes to soothe the bruised egos of his firm's clients.

One day, Eddie Anderson quits. Predictably, his contemporaries are frightened and view him as being out of his mind. His wife attempts to have him certified as insane, and the family lawyer is sent to talk some sense into him. The story of Eddie Anderson, however, is, in the end, the tale of one man's attempt to return to the spirit of his Dream and to rework it into his life, so that he is revitalized by its heart.

Many of us in mid-life, like Anderson, face this developmental challenge when it comes to our Dream: dealing with the disparity between whom we have become and whom we once dreamed of becoming. Having failed to realize our cherished dreams, we must come to terms with our disappointment and settle on new choices around which to build our lives. In reappraising our life, we find ourselves asking: "What is the fate of my youthful Dream? What possibilities exist for change in the future?"

By the time we reach the middle years we also realize, hopefully, that whatever is incomplete in our life is something we have left out. Some of us may have to mourn the person we have not and now will never become. No one, though, escapes consequences at mid-life. Those of us who have realized some of our early dreams, for example, need to consider the meaning and value of that success.

About age forty, then, many of us respond to the call to come home to ourselves. In reworking our Dream, we grieve some of our life choices, directions taken, and mistakes made. This process of mourning helps us to commit ourselves eventually to a life structure within which we can live during the following stable period. Others of us will need to formulate a new life Dream to serve us during life's second half. Having brought our original Dream to fruition, we commit ourselves to a new framework, one that will be a center of passion for us. Still others of us will recommit ourselves to the structures within which we lived during our thirties. Even those of us who go back to previous life structures will find that, in addressing the developmental work of the transition at mid-life, those structures have been somewhat affected. Although they may appear to be the same, in reality they are different.

One mid-life woman religious, for example, experienced a particularly turbulent transition around age forty. She found herself plagued by serious doubts about her vocation and previous life choices. With the help of friends and a spiritual guide, however, she spent these transitional years reworking her self-understanding and appreciation of religious life. As she moved toward the end of her forties, she decided to recommit herself to her congregation.

If we met this woman first at age forty, however, and then again ten years later we might think initially that not much had changed in her life during the past decade. After all, she would appear to be living in much the same way as when we first encountered her: in a community with other sisters and engaged in the ministry of education. If we took time, though, to talk with her about her journey of recent years, we would find that she is a very different person because of her hard work during a time of life transition. We would discover, too, that her life structure has also been transformed: relationships and her spiritual life have become more central.

2. Re-formulating identity

What's an identity? That feeling of knowing who we are and where our life is going. A solid identity — at any age — is never purchased cheaply. To secure one we must be willing to do three things: explore our options for living, experience crises, and make a commitment. While we face the challenge of forming an identity first of all during the adolescent years, this task re-emerges during any time of life change and transition; mid-life is no exception to this rule.

With that settled, however, this question arises: are there differences between men and women when it comes to forming and reformulating an identity? Quite simply, yes. Men, for example, find that mature intimacy is just not possible without a sense of personal identity. Unless they are at home with themselves, they don't get close to others. If they are unsure of themselves, men will often present an image of extraordinary competence to friends and colleagues. They are, however, less able to share with them their weaknesses, needs, and insecurities. All that must change if the gift of intimacy is to be theirs at mid-life.

Women, in contrast, form their identity through relationships. In relationships, most women come to discover who they are. Connections and relationships are important to most women; separation and autonomy preoccupy most men. While men and women arrive at it in different ways, then, a healthy sense of personal identity is an essential ingredient for both in any relationship of intimacy.

A number of women religious today, however, — particularly those whose formation predates Vatican II — raise this question: Does their process of identity reformulation at mid-life mirror that of men religious more closely than would be expected? Many of these women, for example, point to the fact that they were forced to make a complete break with family and friends when they entered their congregation. Within the community itself relationships were also actively discouraged with warnings about particular friendships to say nothing of relationships with those outside the community, especially men.

Many of these women report that the only justifiable relationships they could nurture were those found in the apostolate or of a helping nature. They could, for example, help the students they taught and their families, or the patients they served in the hospital. They, in turn, were themselves helped by benefactors, spiritual guides, and superiors.

A number of women religious who served in overseas mission indicate that the problem has often been particularly acute: they were uprooted frequently or found themselves set apart by the people they served. At mid-life, these women and others whose formation and congregational rules during their early years of religious life discouraged friendships find themselves struggling to reclaim a very important part of their lives: the world of relationships.

How does identity develop over time? During early adulthood many of us fashion a public self to showcase our skills and talents with an overall goal of winning us approval and insuring success.[34] We rely heavily on external criteria to measure progress made toward that goal. Validation of our worth often gets tied up in superficial indicators: the title of our job, the feats of our children, or some external accomplishment. What is the single greatest problem faced by young people at this time in life? Their failure to understand that setbacks and failures are to be expected and can, in fact, be useful tools for learning.

Early in life, in other words, we have questions about who we are becoming; later on we often wonder who we have become. As mentioned earlier, three elements are necessary in the process of identity formation: exploration, crises, commitment.

Late in adolescence and during our early twenties, we can explore options in several areas: life direction, choice of work, relationships, sexuality, and the spiritual life. Does it surprise you that many of these same areas reemerge for consideration at mid-life?

Crises refer to those times of struggle and questioning during which we rethink old roles and life plans and, perhaps, test out some new ones. The word commitment, in contrast, describes our personal investment in something we have chosen.

Some of us, however, decide early on in life to skip the exploration and crises stages of identity formation. Because of fear, insecurity, the pressure of parents, youthful idealism, or some other factor, we jump into a life commitment quickly and thus foreclose our identity. The outcome is disappointing, and similar to ordering a suit of clothing through the mail. It seldom fits properly. The sleeves are usually a bit too long. The jacket too tight across the chest. A foreclosed identity is much the same: not tailor-made for the person wearing it, it looks as though it was fashioned for someone else.

Those of us who foreclose our identity usually commit ourselves too early. We fail to explore our options for living. Refusing to question, or at least question deeply, our values, beliefs, and goals, we commit ourselves to please authority or some external circumstance.

What do those of us who foreclosed our identity look like as we approach mid-life? Stable, sober, responsible — but lacking in curiosity and independence. Repression is our major defense; unacceptable feelings, such as angry and sexual ones, are pushed out of our awareness. In general, we unquestioningly endorse these values: obedience, strong leadership, respect for authority. We are also passive and maintain strong ties with our parents' outlooks and standards. Our relationships tend to be stereotypical: we are more comfortable relating to others out of a role than as a person. Is there any hope for change? Yes, it goes by the name: the transition at mid-life!

Mid-lifers, however, need to guard against adopting a single fixed identity. While we strive for authenticity, we must also develop multiple identities to respond successfully to the ever changing conditions of life.[35] This approach to life and relationships is not hypocritical, rather it emphasizes one or another aspect of our personality in every relationship and situation we enter. Don't we often enough relate differently at home than at work, and differently again among friends as opposed to some less familiar colleagues? In addition, multiple identities also appear to be excellent buffers against physical and emotional illness.

3. Multi-generational mentoring

Mid-life presents an optimal opportunity to mentor and, thus, expand our care for others. As mentioned in Chapter II, mentors help us face the questions we have about life. Simply stated, they are sponsors and guides. Our relationship with a mentor, however, depends more on mutuality, reciprocity, and friendship than on any directions given by someone who has all the answers.[36] Helpful mentors do not try to make us over into their own image and likeness; rather, they provide us with encouragement and a life worthy of emulation. Neither parents nor peers, mentors have some of the qualities of both. Early in life it is important to have a mentor; at mid-life it is just as important for us to be mentors ourselves.

As implied just above, mentors usually occupy an important place in our lives during early adulthood. First and foremost, they help us to identify the elements of our Dream and encourage us to nurture them and give them a place in our life. Author Edward Sellner puts it this way: mentors bring out the ideals and convictions that are stirring within us. They introduce us to aspects of ourselves of which we are unaware.[37]

Mentors can also aid us as we address the question of our vocation in life: "What is God's Dream for us?" How? By helping us realize that discerning our vocation ultimately means leaving the future in God's hands.[38] As a consequence, theologian Rosemary Haughton calls mentors "agents of transformation."

Mentors provide counsel and support in times of stress and can serve as models by their own achievements and way of life. Sharing a number of elements with other types of love relationships, many mentoring relationships blossom eventually into deep friendships as those of us being mentored gain a fuller sense of our own authority and capabilities. Supporting this point of view is Thomas Merton's description of the spiritual director as an individual to whom we can say "what we really mean in the depths of our souls, not what we think we are expected to say."

Mentors, in other words, speak the language of the heart.[39] Spiritual mentors, in particular, are blessed with this gift; their relationships with others are marked by an unusual depth and have as their focus the spiritual dimensions of life. Mentors must also be willing to share some of the details of their own life journey, along with its joys and trials. They do not have all the answers but rather are fellow seekers of wisdom.

At mid-life, however, the task of mentoring can often enough have an older generation as its target. This second focus is not so clearly defined. Some general guidelines, though, do exist. Mentors can help older people rediscover parts of themselves lost when they made past decisions. In making earlier life choices, all of us, by necessity, neglected parts of our personality. During life's second half we can rediscover these forgotten gifts. Truman Capote's evocative phrase "other voices, other rooms" captures our experience as we listen to and search out parts of ourselves that need to be integrated into our life's fabric.

A bishop, for example, is faced with a sixty-year-old pastor in failing health. Although not completely incapacitated, this older man needs to reduce his workload dramatically. As a mentor, the bishop can help him explore his unrealized talents, early Dream, and the contributions he has made already. The bishop can also help the older man be realistic about his present strengths and abilities. In working together over time, both benefit from their relationship. The bishop mentors the pastor who can assume a position in which he can rediscover his talents and use them for the Church while still caring for his limited health.

Mentors can be especially helpful to those of us who have failed to examine ourselves or make necessary changes during the transitions at mid-life or earlier. We often find the transitions that follow age forty to be times of moderate to severe crisis. Having failed to examine ourselves and make whatever adjustments are necessary, we feel increasingly cornered. Some of us blame others for our dilemma. Mentoring can be an unexpected blessing as we move out of our fourth decade of life. Professional counseling and/or spiritual direction may also be necessary. The support and compassion of a mentor will, however, be essential if we are to address some of the developmental work which we avoided earlier.

4. Refashioning commitments

At mid-life permanent commitments also come up for review. Some of us make these types of promises early in life, others of us delay them, still others make major commitments in some areas of life and not others. We might, for example, settle down into a particular career or line of work but leave our options open when it comes to long-term relationships. Regardless of the pattern we follow, this much is clear: at mid-life we cannot avoid taking a look at this important area of our life.

The task of reviewing permanent commitments, however, should not be carried out in isolation. Along with their spiritual dimension, most life commitments have both individual and interpersonal components. We cannot reassess and renew any commitment adequately without considering the relationships that exist in our life.

A lifelong commitment is a natural way of expressing both the love we have for another and of proving and preserving that love.[40] Permanence is a property of every commitment that flows from and continues in love. A middle-aged woman, for example, who returns home from work one evening and prepares dinner for her tired husband and moody teen-aged brood, may look down the table and ask herself what her life would be like had she not married this man and mothered all these children. Asking this question, however, does not mean necessarily that she will leave the table, go to her bedroom, pack, and set out in search of a new life.

Our relationships, then, are an important ingredient in any process of reworking commitments at mid-life. This fact should not surprise us. After all, isn't the experience of intimacy an ideal preparation for making a commitment? What do we mean by intimacy? James and Evelyn Whitehead frame their definition of the word as a question: *"Am I sure enough of myself and confident enough of my abilities that I can risk closeness with another — i.e., allow another person to come close enough that I could possibly be changed by our relationship?"*[41]

The process of reassessing my permanent commitments at mid-life and reworking my Dream also go hand-in-hand. In the case of the latter, for example, fidelity demands that I give consideration to those to whom I am already committed. They helped me to become the person I am; in their own way, they probably played a role in helping me form my Dream and encouraged me to give it a place of prominence in my life. When my Dream and state in life appear incompatible, I do not necessarily need to change my state in life. To do so may be just a way of avoiding the pain that growth often requires. If any of us changes our life commitments for this type of reason, we will find ourselves facing the same difficulties in later commitments.

One final point about refashioning commitments. At midlife, more so than before, we learn that when it comes to commitments the virtue of fidelity needs to take prominence over perseverance. Commitments are meant to be life giving; they should not be contests of endurance. By the time we reach age forty, we realize that while some commitments can be refreshed or refashioned, others have died and still others should be brought to an end. A great deal of soul searching must always accompany any journey to these last two destinations. It is also important to mourn the passing of any life commitment that has come to an end. Why? Because, similar to the loss suffered in death, something that once gave great life to some people no longer does so.

In addressing the developmental challenges outlined just above, we work more seriously than before on becoming individuals. Psychiatrist Carl Jung called this effort the process of *individuation* and highlighted two important aspects of it: the limited growth of many of us during early adulthood and the unique opportunities that we have for human development at mid-life. He observed that in spite of the changes we go through during our twenties and thirties, a number of us arrive at midlife not much different from the person we were in our early twenties.

Jung put it this way: "Wholly unprepared, we set out upon the second half of life. Worse still, we take this step with the false assumption that our truths and ideals will serve us as hitherto. But we cannot live the afternoon of life according to the program of life's morning: for what was great in the morning will be little at evening, and what in the morning was true will at evening have become a lie."[42] The transition at mid-life gives us another chance to make more serious life changes and to chart new directions. The work of becoming an individual is expedited when we pursue the tasks of developing, reconciling, and integrating our various polarities. We do not undertake this effort, however, for the sake of self-fulfillment; no, as mentioned at the outset of Chapter II, by mid-life we understand more fully that the goal of psychological and spiritual growth is self-transcendence. Stated simply, those of us who complete the work of the transition well realize that fundamental to our human growth is the awareness of our communion with one another.

What, then, is important at mid-life? Befriending your real self, coming to grips with personal mortality, mentoring the next generation — and the one ahead of you if necessary, reworking your life Dream and sense of identity, transcending yourself.

In Chapter VI we'll see that deepening friendships is another important task at mid-life as is finding God in surprising places and dealing with life-long angers. To accomplish these ends, however, we must pursue the task of developing, reconciling, and integrating our various polarities. At the start of Chapter VI we will define the word archetype; that word will also help us clarify our use of the term polarity. Right now, though, move on to this Chapter's *Reflection Questions* and the essay entitled *Desert Days* found in Chapter V.

REFLECTION QUESTIONS

Listed below are three questions that may help you apply the material in this chapter to your own life. Find a quiet place and reflect on these questions and your response to each one. You may want to make a few notes for later review and to participate more fully in any future discussion.

1. At mid-life many of us confront mortality for the very first time. Illness, the death of a parent or friend, the experience of aging — all can trigger a confrontation with mortality. What did the same for you during the middle years? How has the realization that you have probably lived already more years than the number that lie ahead brought about a change in outlook?

2. Spend some time thinking about your life's Dream. What are some of its elements and how have you, or have you not, given them a place in your life? Did that early Dream "fire you up"? As you grew older, how did you find a way to restore fire and passion to your life? By reworking your life's Dream? By finding a new one? Please explain.

3. Identify at least one mentor who helped you during your early adult years. Name this person and describe those aspects of the relationship that helped you identify your life's Dream and to give that Dream a place in your life. In looking back on your twenties and thirties, perhaps you cannot identify a mentor. How has this lack of one affected you during those formative years?

4. Mid-life is a time in life to be a mentor. How is that statement true for you? What factors impede you from taking on this important task at mid-life?

5. One mid-life man, in the midst of an age forty transition, had this to say, "Sometimes I feel like an eighteen-year-old again. I am asking at forty the same questions I asked more than two decades ago: 'Who am I?' 'Where am I going in life?'" Have you ever found yourself doing the very same thing?

6. Some people at mid-life feel as though they are going crazy. They do not seem to know who they are anymore. Can you identify with them? Spend some time considering the ways in which your sense of identity has grown and changed over time. What led to the changes? What was the experience of change like?

NOTES

[13] Tobias Wolff, *In Pharaoh's Army: Memories of the Lost War* (New York, NY: Alfred A. Knopf, 1994), p. 220.

[14] Sheehy, *New Passages*, p. 58.

[15] *Ibid.*, pp. 63, 274.

[16] L. Patrick Carroll, SJ and Katherine Marie Dyckman, SNJM, *Chaos or Creation: Spirituality at Mid-life* (New York: Paulist Press, 1986), p. 26.

[17] Sheehy, *New Passages*. p. 63.

[18] *Ibid.*, pp. 67-134.

[19] *Ibid.*, p. 255.

[20] Samuel Osherson, *Finding our Fathers: The Unfinished Business of Manhood* (New York: The Free Press, 1986).

[21] Lillian Rubin, *Intimate Strangers: Men and Women Together* (New York: Harper and Row, 1983), pp. 120-159.

[22] Sheehy, *New Passages*, pp. 221-222.

[23] *Ibid.*

[24] Sean D. Sammon, "The Meaning of 'Meaning It'," ed. Joseph L. Hart, *Fidelity* (Whitinsville, MA: Affirmation Books), pp. 19-48.

[25] James Zullo, "The Crisis of Limits: Mid-life Beginnings," *Human Development* (3) 1, 1982, pp. 2-10.

[26] Howell Raines, *Fly Fishing Through the Mid-life Crisis* (New York: Morrow, 1993).

[27] Sheehy, *New Passages*, p. 205.

[28] The data in this paragraph is a summary of findings cited by Sheehy, p. 298.

[29] *Ibid.*, p. 208.

[30] *Ibid.*, p. 221.

[31] *Ibid.*, p. 146.

[32] Elia Kazan, *The Arrangement* (New York: Stein, 1967).

[33] Kazan, *The Arrangement*.

[34] Sheehy, *New Passages*, pp. 52-53.

[35] *Ibid.*, p. 71.

[36] Edward C. Sellner, *Mentoring: The Ministry of Spiritual Kinship* (Notre Dame, IN: Ave Maria Press, 1990), p. 10.

[37] *Ibid.*, pp. 19-20.

[38] *Ibid.*, p. 49.

[39] *Ibid.*, p. 57.

[40] John Haughey, *Can Anyone Say Forever* (Garden City, NY: Doubleday, 1975), p. 57.

[41] James D. and Evelyn E. Whitehead, *Christian Life Patterns* (Garden City, NY: Doubleday, 1979), pp. 71-111.

[42] Carl Jung, *Modern Man in Search of a Soul*, trans. W.S. Dell and Cary F. Baynes (New York: Harcourt, Brace and World, 1933), p. 108.

CHAPTER V

DESERT DAYS

A phone call brought the news. "My cancer is back," she said. Four simple words with the power to end your life. Twice before she had battled this elusive killer and won. This time, though, we both knew the outcome could be different. I asked myself: "Has she called this morning to tell me that she is getting ready to die?"

Shocking news? Not really. How often had we talked about the cancer's return, as though it was away at school. Over a drink at night, on the phone, or while walking one of those quiet English roads that have, for centuries, eavesdropped on similar conversations, we talked about that possibility becoming an eventuality, and, perhaps — finally — a reality.

Death stalks us at mid-life. We realize, of course, that it's always been there, lurking in the shadows. But about mid-life it becomes more brazen, overpowering some, bringing them down quickly. Others of us are more fortunate: death will follow us at a distance for some years to come, awaiting another moment and opportunity to make its move.

Early in life, young and half-formed, we foolishly nourish ourselves with this innocent assurance: of all people ever born we are invincible. That's right, invincible; death will call on others but not on us. The middle years teach us otherwise, and for some it is a very bitter lesson indeed.

When death threatens to visit early in life's afternoon, you question God's wisdom and sense of fair play; all the more so when it plans to call in on someone you love. I know I did. "Where is this God of mine," I asked at first, "the one I hardly know anymore?" In retrospect I'm not surprised that a short time later I stopped praying. What robbed me of any desire for God? All the recent mid-life loss and death? Not really — I wasn't angry, just strangely indifferent.

You see, the God of my imagination disappeared in my forty-sixth year. My response? I put out a missing person's report and refused to accept this troubling fact: the God I knew, had known since I was a child, simply did not exist and never had. In time I came to see that the God of my life's morning was hardly God at all.

God missing and my heart without a spark to ignite a prayer — "Is this," I mused, "the world of mid-life spiritual-ity?" How like that image of the dry well. For so long my prayer had been arid, hopeless, filled with impatient waiting. All those methods used to start again when before I'd gone astray in prayer also failed to work. Eventually this painful lesson was hammered home: faced with a dry well, you have no choice but to sit and wait for the rain — patiently. When did it come for me? After my heart and understanding had changed enough that I began to see correctly and realize that mid-life and its losses were God's means for re-creating me.

Looking back I'm embarrassed to say I never caught the fact that God was trying to get my notice. Have you ever failed to see an object right in front of you because you expect to find it someplace else? I was busy looking for God in the usual places — but God had moved, without leaving a forwarding address.

God has this much in common with death: both wait patiently before making their move. Death knows that time is on its side and so does God — after all, isn't God's timeline eternity? My friend's mid-life illness made me want to pray. Not that this God of ours needed my prayers. "Pray if you must," I thought, "but do so without illusion and do it for yourself." That's right, pray because it benefits you; much as a tender conversation with a new friend strengthens the fragile bond between you both. Prayer consoled me, not God. Mercifully, it consoled my friend, too. A mix of prayer and medical science: two ingredients for health. She is better now; her will to fight is back. While the outcome of her illness is as yet unknown, she now has hope. Hope — the virtue that helps us all to believe there is a dawn just over the horizon, even on the bleakest of days.

What do you do when you realize that the God of your life's morning is hardly God at all? I went out to the desert one night and spent time with the stars. The desert is, of course, the only place on earth where you can really see them without distraction. There in my personal planetarium I let their beauty and vastness wash over me. Can a God who made all these, I asked, really take an interest in me? Before long I had my answer: looking on us with love is something that comes naturally to this God of ours.

With the suddenness that the God of my life's morning had disappeared, another was born in my forty-seventh year. Or was it the other way around: was it I who was born anew in God? This one, though, wanted to be my lover and not some harmless, simple soul to whom I would periodically attend.

Young and new at making love we often play on that border between the land of pleasure and of pain, confusing our partner and ourselves. Mid-life love making is more mature: the satisfying excitement of sharing passion and play with one who is ever familiar and yet always new. Yes, that's what God was offering — the God who took my hand and led me into that desert land to view the stars. The target of God's affections? My heart. This time I took a chance and surrendered. At Emmaus didn't the hearts of two disciples burn? For me, nearly two millennia later, I knew the outcome could only be the same.

At mid-life God taught me that the desert is a fertile place. But first my sight and understanding had to change. Vast, foreign, dry, hot and cold sandwiched within the hours of any passing day. Early in life I avoided the desert, judging it barren and unfit for life. Mid-life's uncertainty has reminded me that it's home. Who would want to live there? Here at mid-life I find myself asking: "Who would want to live anywhere else?"

CHAPTER VI

MID-LIFE AND AFTERWARDS

At mid-life we are challenged, once again, to come to grips with the opposing forces in our lives: polarities. What are polarities? Pairs of images established over thousands of generations that come to exist in every person's mind. Each of us, for example, has an understanding of what it means to be young or old aside from the chronological meaning of these words. To be young is to be lively, growing, and heroic but also impulsive and inexperienced. By contrast, being old can mean being wise, influential, and mature, but also at times bitter, demanding, and unconnected to life.[43]

ARCHETYPES FOSTER DEVELOPMENT

Carl Jung used the word archetype to describe polarities, and suggested that archetypes either develop to a high degree or remain dormant. Jung observed that developing one's archetypes is an important part of becoming an individual. They evolve in each of us from rather undifferentiated ideas into increasingly complex internal images, giving us the potential for further development. For instance, when we consider our image of God, we might find — if we have reflected upon it — that God's image in us is much more complex and differentiated during our adult years than it was when we were six or seven years old.

Three of Jung's sets of polarities are important for our discussion: separate-belonging; creative-destructive; and masculine-feminine. The development and integration of the first is necessary for progress in the spiritual life, the second for resolving lifelong angers, and the third is an invisible partner in many relationships.

Separate-belonging

The tasks that make up the transition at mid-life are not only psychological. They are also spiritual. The separate-belonging polarity, for example, enables us to deal with the issues of solitude and attachment. It is important for young adults to achieve membership in their wider society and to be an affirmed part of it. Early in life we need to be accepted by our peers; at midlife, however, it is more important that we understand our own solitude. Many of us fear solitude because our society equates it with loneliness, but these two states are quite different. The lonely person is someone who is alienated from his or her internal resources. More important, in fleeing from solitude we forfeit our chance of discovering many aspects of ourselves and of our life with God.

In contrast, those of us who seek solitude become less dependent on others. We achieve a better balance between our needs and those of society. In attending to ourselves in a way that is not self-centered, we become less controlled by our ambitions and dependencies. Hence, we can be involved in better ways with others and contribute to society in a more selfless manner. Simply stated, to be able to care deeply for others, we must also care deeply for ourselves. This caring, however, concerns itself with human and spiritual development and integrity, rather than with material possessions.

New Understandings and Images Needed

Solitude, then, gives us an opportunity to deepen our spiritual life. Faith is shaped by the initiatives of grace and the Spirit, but the integration of the separate-belonging polarity provides fertile ground for the movement of the Spirit in our lives. At every major life transition, we are presented with the opportunity for developing the new era's life structure and for finding innovative and enriching ways of being in faith. We will fail if we insist on clinging rigidly to our prior understandings of faith and earlier images of God. In developing and integrating the separate-belonging polarity we take an opportunity to complete this task successfully.

Being a spiritual person includes ultimately coming to let God love us on God's terms, not ours. Jesuit Thomas Green, writing in his book *When the Well Runs Dry*, suggests that God's way of loving us may differ from human love.[44] If we mistakenly insist that God love us in a human way, we may miss the extraordinary relationship into which God invites each of us.

To illustrate this point, let's stretch the image used in the title of Green's book mentioned just above. The water in the well is God's consoling grace. Early in the spiritual life, we are young, energetic, strong — the well also brims with water. It is relatively easy for us to take a bucket and satisfy our spiritual thirst with the cool refreshing water of God's consolation.

As we grow older in the spiritual life, however, the water

level drops and our earlier strength diminishes. It becomes harder to get water from the well. With human effort, though, we can still satisfy ourselves with the water of God's grace; that task, however, is not so easy as it was years earlier.

The day will come when we have grown to maturity in the spiritual life and the well will have run dry. What can we do then to share in God's comforting grace? Nothing. That's right, *nothing* — except to sit and wait for the rain. When any of us reaches this point in the spiritual life, we are ready to allow God to love us as God chooses to love us.

How do most of us respond to this situation? By declaring that our prayer is barren, empty, arid. What a remarkable conclusion! Just when God has cleared away the distractions and led us into the wilderness to speak to our heart, we insist that God has abandoned us.

At mid-life all of us face this faith issue: how to respond to God's invitation to new forms of prayer. Old ones, quite frankly, don't work anymore. For some, prayer is deeper and freer of thoughts and images. What must we do to enter into this new form of prayer? Surrender.

Several signs indicate that such an invitation is being extended. First of all, many of us report a growing sense of our need to be redeemed. Now more reliant on God, we are aware of the experience of individual and social sin. Second, some of us find that we can no longer meditate. For others of us, prayer is uneventful and arid: consolation is lacking and old forms of worship are found wanting. These words capture well the mid-life experience of prayer for many of us: "At mid-life, we long for a simple presence before God; *we want only to be free enough to be* with *God,* not think *about* God."

Teresa of Avila apparently faced the same dilemma as many of us. Her solution, one among many, was simple and summed up her definition of contemplation. She often said that when she was unable to find words for her prayer, she would go into the chapel and sit before the Blessed Sacrament so that the Lord could look on her with love.

Jesuit Green gives us similar advice. Float! — he says. That's right: float! If you've ever been caught in the ocean's undertow, you know that swimming against it is one of the best ways to drown. If, however, you float — in other words, go with the tide — chances are that you'll survive. While the tide may initially take you out into the sea, it will often bring you back eventually to the shore. The same movements mark our prayer. If we fight the changes occurring in prayer at mid-life, we'll miss a wonderful opportunity for a deeper, if initially less familiar, relationship with God. If, on the other hand, we can let God love us on God's terms — well, we will have given ourselves a wonderful mid-life gift.

CREATIVE-DESTRUCTIVE

The creative-destructive polarity, and its resolution have implications for the angers of our lifetime. We all have the power to be creative and also to injure and destroy others intentionally or unintentionally. In life we will hurt others and will in turn be hurt by them. During the transition at mid-life we have an opportunity to come to terms with this fact and with our grievances against others for perceived injustices and especially for the disappointments we've experienced. This task involves a process of mourning and letting go.

What happens if we fail to undertake this journey at mid-life? We run the risk of continuing a romance with perceived injustices and genuine disappointments. For example, by mid-life many of us realize that life can be unfair. Some people are killed in war, others never go. Some are blessed with intellectual or athletic abilities, many of their age-mates are not. During our middle years, we feel a growing urgency to find an answer to this question: "How can we deal with life's inevitable disappointments?"

The same principle holds true when we consider the ways in which we have been hurt by others. Has anyone, for example, ever related to you the details of an injustice done to him or her? Listening to the person's tale and witnessing his or her obvious rage, you are sure the event took place just recently. Later, you discover that the situation occurred fifteen years ago and that most of those involved are dead!

Some of us come to mid-life and find that we have trophy cases full of injustices, and gladly display them to anyone who shows the slightest interest. Nurturing these perceived injustices, though, saps us of our creative energy. Eventually, we become mired in rage. Our energy and creativity are dissipated by our self-righteous indignation. As "angry martyrs," ultimately we have turned our destructiveness on ourselves.

To flourish at mid-life we need to integrate our creative-destructive sides. A middle-aged factory worker, for example, believes that he is well suited to be the shop steward at a particular plant. He is quick to point out that he has the necessary experience and seniority for the position. This man's supervisor, however, has a dilemma. He knows full well that if he appoints him shop steward, he will have to find a number of new workers for the plant. Experience notwithstanding, the man seeking the job does not get along well with others.

So, what to do? The supervisor decides to appoint another worker as shop steward. *It is the right decision, but he has acted in a manner that some of us might term destructive.* However unintentionally, the supervisor has hurt someone. False understandings about the virtue of charity cause some of us, early in life, to avoid making hard decisions like the supervisor's in our example. This type of avoidance does not ultimately help anyone. Charity, in the case of our example, also calls us to speak out of an attitude of loving concern with the man who did not get the job. Stated simply, we should tell him the truth — not necessarily all the truth, all at once — but nevertheless — the truth.

What about that man who was disappointed because someone else got the position he wanted? Speaking forthrightly with him about the situation and its details may not resolve it for him. It may, however, offer the possibility of new life springing from the soil of his hurt. He'd be well advised, for example, to express his disappointment and anger. By so doing, he increases the possibility of surfacing underlying fears about incompetence and rejection. Mistaken notions about anger, however, cause many of us to deny or repress this feeling. The vast majority of us have just not been taught how to fight fairly. If we fail to deal with our feelings of anger and disappointment, they go underground and fester. At mid-life we need to learn skills that will help us do otherwise.

Masculine-feminine

Psychologist Carol Gilligan once summarized the reasons for the inevitable misunderstandings between men and women in this way, "It all goes back, of course, to Adam and Eve, a story which shows, among other things, that if you make a woman out of a man, you are bound to get into trouble."[45] Men and women are different in a number of ways. Many women, for example, focus on the necessary interdependence of us all. In contrast, the majority of men make autonomy and independence the priority. Care on the part of others can be experienced as interference.

Developing further the differences between men and women, Michael McGill, Professor of Organizational Behavior and Administration at Southern Methodist University, suggests that men usually come together around something.[46] The bonds they develop often have more to do with solidarity than with self-disclosure. Early in life, for example, most men learn how to be part of a team. In adulthood, teamwork continues to be important for them, on the job, or when they get together to work out, or to play golf or tennis. It's the things that men do together that bind them. Often enough, if you take away those things, men stop coming together.

Women are different. Their relationships with other women are usually more important than anything they might do together. Psychologist Lillian Rubin reminds us that most women value their friendships with other women especially for the emotional support and encouragement they receive.[47]

To illustrate the differences between men and women in the areas of self-disclosure and relationships, McGill offers this common example. If a woman calls a woman and says, "Let's go to lunch," the other woman usually replies, "When?" If a man calls another man, however, and says, "Let's go to lunch," the response will be most likely, "Why?"

The differences between men and women are perhaps best illustrated, though, in the friendships they form with one another. Expectations about emotional sharing and sexual attraction can easily lead to confusion. Some men feel pressured by a woman friend to reveal more of themselves than is comfortable for them. In contrast, many women are disappointed that their male friends are not so forthcoming in their emotional sharing as they would like them to be. They find themselves saying, "I never know what's going on with him."

With all that said, however, Jung emphasizes this important fact: we are all androgynous, having both a masculine and a feminine side.[48] Among women, the masculine side is often unconscious. The same may be said of many a man's feminine side. If we are all androgynous, though, why does that important fact appear to elude so many of us until mid-life? Jungian analyst and Episcopal priest John Sanford cites a number of reasons. First of all, he points out that some of us give little importance to self-knowledge early in life. Faced with emotional confusion and pain, we choose to live meaningless lives rather than come to know ourselves better.

Next, some aspects of ourselves defy greater self-knowledge. These shadow traits, often obvious to others, are hidden from us. The Gospels, for example, remind us about the man who saw the beam in his neighbor's eye but failed to see the one in his own. Even though our shadow side is apparent to everyone else, we are often the last to know about it.

Finally, we lack knowledge of our unconscious masculine or feminine side because we typically project it onto others. Projecting some aspect of ourselves onto others makes it look as though it has little to do with us. Consider the example of the overhead projector and screen. The transparency containing the information we plan to present is set on a projector; resting on top, it looks as though it is part of the machine. Once the projector is turned on, the material on the transparency gets projected onto the screen. The transparency with its information, however, still rests on the projector.

When we project some aspect of ourselves, it is perceived as being outside ourselves, as though it pertained to someone else but had little or nothing to do with us. The reality of the other person becomes obscured by the projection, and he or she becomes either over- or undervalued.

If a man who has failed to integrate his masculine and feminine sides, for example, forms a relationship with a woman, he will often enough project the positive aspects of his feminine side onto her. As a consequence, she become highly desirable to him and is the object of his erotic fantasies and sexual longings. He will come to believe that he would be fulfilled if only he could make love to her. This situation eventually becomes suffocating for the woman involved. As she attempts to develop her own personality, she finds that her partner begins to project the negative parts of his unconscious feminine side onto her and begins to blame her for his moods and unhappiness. Why so? He has been relating to a projection and not a real person.

Similarly, a woman who lacks integration of her feminine-masculine polarity will often enough project positive aspects of her unconscious masculine side onto a man. When this occurs she comes to view him as a guide, hero, or savior and feels that she can be complete only through him. Once the relationship is viewed realistically, however, her hero becomes an infuriating and frustrating man responsible for many of her disappointments and feelings of being belittled. Situations involving projection have very little to do with actual love or intimacy. Instead, they are states of mutual fascination and infatuation. Real love is between real people, not projections.

Relationships of Intimacy

To establish a relationship of mature intimacy, our masculine and feminine aspects must achieve a certain level of integration. Early in life, however, this type of integration is often missing. Why? Unsure of ourselves, we find it difficult to be vulnerable enough to let others come close in a relationship so that we could be changed. As a consequence, many of us — perhaps especially men, are not ready for a genuine relationship of intimacy until at least mid-life. Let's explore that notion a bit more.

Looking back on our lives, a number of us realize that as we approached the end of our twenties relationships of intimacy took on greater importance. Feeling more secure in some areas of life — work, to name just one — we turned our attention to others. Some of us also had a deep experience of love somewhere along the road between our late twenties and early thirties. It was an important first step toward the type of loving relationships that are one mark of mature adulthood.

At mid-life we begin to realize that developing and integrating our masculine-feminine polarity will help us understand better and discard the sexual stereotypes that can dominate the early part of our lives. The process of integration also enhances the possibility of developing relationships of intimacy in our life.

Addressing the first reason, we note immediately that the terms masculine and feminine refer to the meaning of gender and not to biological gender. Every culture has its gender images. In the U.S., for example, little boys are still taught not to cry, while some teenage girls are encouraged subtly to deny their natural intellectual abilities when they threaten a romantic relationship. The indoctrination with gender images begins very early.

Rigid adherence to such stereotypes can give rise to skewed psychological and emotional development. Totally masculine men, for example, are usually unable to be emotionally close to women: they regard them as either maternal or sexual, but not both. The stereotypical woman is presented as either seductive or dependent. These characterizations suggest a failure to develop and reconcile the masculine-feminine polarity.

INTEGRATION REQUIRED FOR INTIMACY

The second reason for developing and integrating the masculine-feminine polarity — to enhance the possibility for relationships of intimacy — is quite important. The transition at midlife appears to provide an optimal set of circumstances in which to address this challenge successfully. In early adulthood, for example, men often experience their feminine side as dangerous, while women do not want to be thought of as too masculine.[49] Young women may shrink from expressing their natural assertiveness and competence because their masculine side is too threatening to them and to others, while young men fear the implications of their more intuitive and relational qualities.

When we have come face-to-face with personal mortality, we appear less concerned about the demands of gender images. Simply put, we are more willing to be ourselves. Before this happens, younger men may keep an emotional distance from women because closeness reminds them of their own feminine side. Along the same lines, many women keep an emotional distance from men because to come too close is also to come face to face with their own masculine side.

In American society today, some people first encounter one another genitally before coming to know each other in a broader and deeper sense. They may be comfortable with genital and physical intimacy, but are less experienced with the harder yet more rewarding work of psychological, emotional, and spiritual intimacy. "Falling in love," or infatuation, is only a step toward intimacy. When the infatuation dissolves and the other person emerges as he or she really is, then — and only then — is true intimacy possible. In an intimate relationship, we accept responsibility for our happiness or unhappiness. We neither expect another person to make us happy nor blame the other for our frustrations, or problems.

The experience of intimacy is an optimal one for discovering our masculine and feminine sides. At mid-life, for example, a number of men begin to discover that their relationships teach them about the importance of intimacy and care of others. Many women have known these realities for a very long time. In another example, a number of middle-aged women, as mentioned earlier, stop trying in their relationships to be selfless. They learn that to discount themselves is self-destructive. Early in life, many women judge themselves in light of their ability to care for others. By mid-life, however, a number of them begin to question if the best way to sustain relationships is solely through the care of other people. Each of these women starts to realize that she is one of the people it is important not to hurt.

A failure to integrate the masculine-feminine polarity gives rise to many problems in relationships.[50] Sanford, for example, points out that a man who lacks integration can appear sulky, overly sensitive, and withdrawn. He acts peevish and depressed, and is unavailable for any satisfying relationship.[51] Sarcasm marks his speech; what passes for humor is often nothing more than innuendo and poisonous jabs.

Women lacking in integration of their masculine-feminine polarity can appear critical and judgmental. Their opinions, however, do not spring from their own process of thinking and feeling. Rather, they have been picked up from various sources: parents, church, authorities, books and articles. If these negative traits get projected onto others, the result is a woman who is blunt and often critical. Eventually, her style of relating saps her of any creativity; others avoid her, and she begins to feel as though she has nothing to offer anyone else.

THE MASCULINE-FEMININE
POLARITY AND GAY AND LESBIAN PERSONS

How, you might ask, does this model apply to homosexually-oriented men and women? In much the same way as it applies to their heterosexual counterparts. In Episcopal priest John Sanford's examples mentioned above, of difficulties in relationships between heterosexually-oriented men and women, he cites a lack of integration of the masculine and feminine as the culprit. Just as many heterosexually-oriented persons have achieved considerable integration when it comes to this polarity, so also a number of homosexually-oriented men and women have accomplished the same task.

The reverse is also true. If a homosexually-oriented man or woman finds that he or she has one experience of infatuation after another, he or she must ask where the lack of integration lies. We said earlier that infatuation can be a step on the road to intimacy. However, if we withdraw from every relationship when the glow of infatuation wears off and the hard coin of intimacy presents itself — at mid-life or any other time, whether heterosexually- or homosexually-oriented, we must look to a failure to integrate our respective masculine and feminine sides as one possible source of this problem with relationships.

At mid-life we are more aware of our need to increase the possibility for intimacy with other persons. As we come to accept our masculine and feminine sides and the many dimensions of our human sexuality, we are more capable of genuine intimacy with others; the threat of closeness is lessened. Thus, by integrating this polarity and growing in realistic self-knowledge and acceptance of who we are psychosexually, we prepare ourselves for the developmental tasks of the mature years — late and late, late adulthood.

Developmental Issues Delayed until Mid-life

James and Evelyn Whitehead describe other difficulties that can occur in relationships between men and women at mid-life.[52] Let's consider men as an example. Some of them come to age forty still carrying with them an adolescent fear of women. This reaction is rooted in a failure to complete some of the developmental tasks of the first four decades of life. Just why is this so?

During our adolescent years, as we come to know who we are and who we are not, sex and sexuality become increasingly more important. Adolescent males, for example, establish their gender identity — their sense of being a man — by setting themselves apart from those who are not male. Hence, through a process of distancing, women come to be experienced as different or "other," especially when it comes to their sexuality.[53]

For some adolescent males, however, women are not only different, they are also dangerous. Why? Because they set off powerful new sexual impulses in the young man, impulses over which he feels little control. The experience of many young men as they grow to identify themselves as adults, then, includes the sense that women are other, different, and — for some — dangerous because of their sexuality.

How do most adolescent males work through this dilemma? By falling in love or going to school with or working alongside women. A romantic experience during the adolescent years brings a young man into a relationship with a *particular* woman. Now an individual person, she is no longer a category. Over time, he discovers that she is more like him as a human being than different. This experience introduces the young adolescent male to the fact that women — rather than being different — are more similar to him than anything else.

A young man's growing ability to see women as persons

and to experience them as individuals is fundamental for healthy relationships between men and women in adult life. Over time he realizes that there are some women whom he likes and others whom he does not — just as there are men for whom he has affection and others for whom he does not.

If a young man does not have the opportunity, however, to fall in love with particular women or to work alongside others, he may continue to see them as a category rather than as individuals. This lack of opportunity has been the lot of some mid-life men in religious life and priesthood. Having failed to come to know individual women, at mid-life they may still relate to members of the opposite sex as different and dangerous.

LATE AND LATE, LATE ADULTHOOD

Death is inevitable, but the manner in which we age is not. The years between the transition at mid-life and our death can span one or several decades. Opportunities for development and growth continue throughout this entire period. In general, we also face initially three developmental tasks: growing in interiority, expanding our capacity to care for others, and developing greater effectiveness in our life's mission.[54] Let's take a look at how we can address these developmental challenges.

Social and personal changes intensify our movement toward interiority. For many of us, this process of "coming home" to ourselves began during the transition at mid-life. Mentoring helps us expand our care for others as we age and to develop greater effectiveness in mission. What exactly do we mean by "mission"? The Gospel assures us of our universal call to holiness, regardless of our vocation in life. And we all do have a vocation: it is God's Dream for us. In light of this call, our mission comes down to these two elements: preaching good news to every creature and growing in compassion. As the social world of older adults changes, they also need to adopt new roles, make former roles more flexible, maintain their health, and compensate for any decline in physical vigor.

During the mature years many of us find ourselves asking: "Does life have any meaning? What will it add up to? Is this what I will be remembered for? Is it too late to put more meaning into my life before I am old?" In attempting to answer these questions, we discover that life has meaning only if our individual lives have meaning. We come also to learn that as we get older it becomes more difficult to lie to ourselves. Naomi Golan, former Dean of the School of Social Work at the University of Haifa, tells us that the transition into late adulthood has three distinct parts: leaving middle adulthood, crossing the line, and entering late adulthood.[55]

1. Leaving middle adulthood

In leaving middle adulthood, we undergo a period of life evaluation. Knowing full well by now that we have lived more years than the number that lie ahead, we question whether or not we have achieved our life's goals. During this first stage of the transition into late adulthood, we also prepare for the inevitable decline that accompanies age by simplifying our lifestyle and reflecting more immediately on what it means to die.

A woman, for example, on turning sixty-five knows that she is closer to death than at forty. She may live for many more years, but at this point in her life she finds that her questions about life's meaning take on a new urgency. Thoughts about death usually lead to questions about what it means to have lived. In addressing them, this woman will have to face the chief developmental task of the period: living with integrity or giving way to despair.

What do we mean by living with integrity? Judging that my life, with all its similarities to the lives of others as well as its idiosyncratic joys and disappointments, could not have been otherwise. Coming to late adulthood, most of us have regrets about what we have or have not done with our lives. Integrity does not eliminate them. Rather, it helps us live in the face of them. During life's second half, for example, the Irish poet Yeats discovered a willingness to forgive himself and "to cast out remorse." By freeing himself from his guilt and regrets about life, he achieved a new sense of well-being.[56]

In contrast, despair describes the false belief that insufficient time remains to start another life or to try out alternative roads to integrity. Those of us who suffer from despair will often say, "If I only knew then what it is that I know now, I most certainly would have lived a different life." Also, if we have avoided work over time on the developmental tasks of life, during late adulthood "the chickens come home to roost." We judge our life unacceptable, complain over the shape of the past, and are unhappy over our present situation. While a metanoia is always possible, knowing that little time is left to us, our dissatisfactions with life can deteriorate into despair.

Psychiatrist George Vaillant[57] points out that among older men an ability to handle life's accidents and conflicts without passivity, blaming, or bitterness is a much better predictor of their mental health during life's later years than a stable childhood. For those of us who have attempted to face the developmental work of previous years, there is growth in integrity and wisdom during the mature years. We find ourselves accepting our lives and those persons important to us as something that had to be, that made us who we are, and that of necessity would permit no substitutes. We present to the coming generation a vital example of a life lived well. Erikson put it this way: "If an older generation has integrity enough to overcome eventually its fear of death, then a younger generation will be unafraid to face life."

Late adulthood can be a period of tremendous spiritual growth. It is usually the old who show younger generations the adequacy of their culture. The real fear of death is usually more the fear of loss of meaning than loss of life. If particular life commitments and ways of living can support people well over the course of life, the value and significance of those commitments and ways of living are confirmed.

Successful aging in late adulthood is marked by a deeper appreciation for the complexity of human life. Psychologist Thomas Moore observes in his best-selling book, *Care of the Soul*, that, "Often care of the soul means not taking sides when there is a conflict at a deep level. It may be necessary to stretch the heart wide enough to embrace contradiction and paradox."[58] These three traits are also important predictors of smooth functioning as we get older: dependability, good organization, and pragmatism.[59] For men, however, the presence of two factors appears to determine whether or not they will have a positive outlook on life. Men who report a strong sense of well-being also experience the comfort of mature love in their life and continue to be excited about living.[60]

Women who report vitality in later life are direct and unaffected in manner.[61] Similar to well-adjusted older men, they also take time to nurture their spiritual life. Focusing their energies on a few well-ordered priorities, these women have a keen interest in giving something back to life. Understandably, this approach to living requires both a firm commitment to the present and plans for the future. Most striking but, perhaps, not surprising: older women who live with a measure of zest

acknowledge the need for some type of physical intimacy —
with friends, grandchildren, other young people. Touch is very
important to them.

For some, late adulthood provides us with the first opportunity in years to play. Life after mid-life can help to reawaken
our curiosity about life, often shelved during earlier periods of
development because of the press of other responsibilities. The
end result of this exciting change is the rediscovery of the play-
ful child in us. We learn to take ourselves less seriously.

2. Crossing the line

Retirement from work, or the reduction of responsibilities for those of us who work in the home, is the single most
important event moving us over the line from middle to late
adulthood. To complete the process well, we must surrender
or adapt some old and familiar roles and adopt some new ones.
For retirement to take place smoothly, we do well to begin our
preparation several years before this event gets underway. We
also need to address these three developmental tasks: first, recognize retirement as a future possibility and begin to shape our
future with it in mind; second, start to take active steps to prepare for the event; third, make a formal decision about when
we will retire and how we will do it. Retirement is a transitional
process; we need to be sure to give ourselves the time we need
to address the task well.

3. Adjusting to the time after retirement

Retirement should not be equated with the cessation of
work. Such a narrow definition fails to recognize the varied activities in which many retired men and women engage. A number of myths about health and the incidence of death just after

retirement also need to be challenged. Retired people, for example, generally maintain their level of health *after* they stop working at their usual job. Retirement also does not appear to have any direct effect on mortality nor on the frequency of social and psychological problems among older men and women.

Some people adjust well to the time after retirement. Others do not. Golan tells us that among those who adjust well, three types stand out: the *mature*, the *rocking-chair*, and the *armored* retirees.[62] The first group move easily into old age. Relatively free of neurotic conflict, they accept themselves realistically and get genuine satisfaction from their activities and personal relationships. Likewise, rocking-chair retirees are generally passive and welcome the opportunity to be free of responsibility. This last advantage more than compensates for any disadvantages that old age might bring. Finally, men and women who have difficulty facing passivity or helplessness in late adulthood can be called the armored type of retiree. Rather than feel sorry for themselves, they keep active in an attempt to ward off their dread of physical decline.

Having lived with integrity, those of us who live on into late, late adulthood find ourselves capitalizing on the unique opportunities provided during this time in life to continue to confront, know, and accept ourselves. We also face three tasks as we make this next transition: coping with impaired health; making adjustments in our living situation so as to provide for any needed care; dealing with the increasing frequency of death among friends and relatives.

Living into late, late adulthood we discover that it too is another time for conversion. James and Evelyn Whitehead remark that these years allow men and women to celebrate the "sacrament of uselessness." We begin to understand more deeply that it is not what we have done or can do that is important. No, it is who we have become that merits recognition.

While we must let go of old self-understandings during late, late adulthood, new ones come to take their place. Death, surely closer than at mid-life or even a few years earlier, again causes us to make some assessments. Life's meaning is more apparent, the consequences of our decisions more clear. As we complete the work of this period, we come to understand more fully one of life's most significant learnings: at the heart of human growth is Christianity's central paradox, the need to die in order to rise anew.

REFLECTION QUESTIONS

Please spend a few moments considering the following questions. They may help you make the material in this chapter your own. Once again, you may want to make a few notes for later reference.

1. Consider your relationships here at mid-life. Write down the names of those whom you hold dear at this time in your life. What makes them so precious? How is the nature of these relationships different from those of life's morning? Try to chart the changes that have occurred in these relationships over the course of life; what gave rise to these changes? Ask yourself this question: "Am I happier in my relationships today than I was fifteen years ago?"

2. What lifelong hurts need to be healed in you? Make a list of them, describing each in detail. Consider the persons involved, the circumstances that gave rise to these hurts. Now ask yourself, "What benefit do I gain by holding on to these hurts? What interferes with my ability to let them go? What can I do to remove those

factors that cause me to hold on to past injustices and disappointments?"

3. Describe your mid-life experience of prayer. Now ask yourself, "Has my life of prayer changed in any appreciable way during my middle years?" If so, in what ways? What led to these changes?

NOTES

[43] Levinson, *Seasons*, pp. 209-221.

[44] Thomas Green, *When the Well Runs Dry* (Notre Dame, IN: Ave Maria Press, 1979).

[45] Carol Gilligan, "Sexes: Attuned to Different Voices," *Washington Post*, January 11, 1983 (Carol Krucoff's interview with Carol Gilligan).

[46] Michael McGill, *The McGill Report on Male Intimacy* (New York: Holt, Rinehart and Winston, 1985).

[47] Lillian Rubin, *Just Friends: The Role of Friendship in our Lives* (New York, NY: Harper and Row, 1985).

[48] Carl Jung, *Letters*, Vol. I (Princeton, NJ: Princeton University Press, 1973), p. 443.

[49] John Sanford, *The Invisible Partners* (New York: Paulist Press, 1980), pp. 56-79.

[50] *Ibid.*, pp. 31-55.

[51] *Ibid.*, pp. 39-43.

[52] James D. and Evelyn E. Whitehead, *Seasons of Strength* (Garden City, NY: Doubleday, 1986), pp. 184-200.

[53] *Ibid.*, pp. 186-199.

[54] James and Evelyn Whitehead, *Christian Life Patterns*, *op. cit.*, pp. 135-190.

[55] Naomi Golan, *Passing Through Transitions: A Guide for Practitioners* (New York: Free Press, 1981), pp. 190-211.

[56] Cited in John Dunne, *The Search for God in Time and Memory* (New York: Macmillan, 1969), pp. 159-160.

[57] George E. Vaillant and Caroline O. Vaillant, "Natural History of Male Psychological Health, a 45-year Study of Predictors of Successful Aging at 65," *The American Journal of Psychiatry*, vol. 147 (January 1990), pp. 31-37.

[58] Thomas Moore, *Care of the Soul* (New York: Harper-Collins, 1992), p. 14.

[59] Vaillant and Vaillant, "Natural History of Male Psychological Health," *op. cit.*, pp. 31-37.

[60] Sheehy, *New Passages*, pp. 384-385.

[61] *Ibid.*, p. 424.

[62] Golan, *Passing Through Transitions*, pp. 204-205.

CHAPTER VII

TESTOSTERONE TRIALS

*O*ne night, three years ago, I popped this question over supper: "I've been without an erection for a year. Is that normal for mid-life?" My query stopped the meal. Stunned silence was the first response, followed by this decisive judgment: "Of course, it's normal." Then, with obvious relief, at least one fellow middle-aged diner returned to his supper. Later, laboring over the dishes, however, another confided quietly, "It's not normal." I knew, of course, that the truth lay here.

Mid-life illness can be a surprising thief. It stole away my sexual energy. Along with that went fire and passion and so much more. What consolation can anyone offer when, at age forty-five, your sexuality lies down and goes to sleep? Is this the rumored falling off, I wondered, male menopause by another name?

Months later I confided my sad loss to an endocrinologist. "A pituitary tumor has that effect," she said, "it transforms you into a latency period boy." Was that, I asked, why touch no longer made me shiver, even the aches and pains of hard physical work failed to make me feel alive?

Testosterone replacement therapy became my treatment:

male mid-life sexuality captured within the confines of a disposable syringe. Within three short days it catapulted me back from boy to middle-aged man with one unexpected difference. Those embarrassing physiological reactions that plague any teenage male became, once again, my concern. To ease my obvious discomfort, the more ribald among my friends encouraged me to look at the situation's possible brighter side. "Maybe," they said, "you'll discover that adolescence is more fun the second time around; perhaps you can enjoy some of the pleasure without suffering all the shame!"

It was the sexual preoccupation, however, that preoccupied me most. Without doubt, I was afflicted with mid-life fever. There were days when the flesh of any twenty-five-year-old held more appeal than that of the most attractive of my contemporaries. I know: beauty is skin deep. In spite of that old adage, my mind often enough had a mind of its own. At the most inopportune of times, a tide of lusty thoughts would rush ashore, wash over my feet, and splash-up against my frame.

I faced this challenge, too: "What to do with the horniness?" The answer to this innocent question is, of course, a great unspoken secret. People ask it generally out of curiosity. A number of us — single, married, or celibate and all of us wanting to be chaste — fail to answer out of shame. It was Chris' query once during a late night conversation — the type that gets underway about day's end and ends just before dawn. We hope we cope differently with horniness at forty-five or six than at sixteen. I know I did.

Because for me, mid-life illness and its cure was also a skillful midwife. Having given my sexuality a second "wake-up call," she taught me three simple lessons. One, it's "OK" to be celibate and chaste, even when the reasons often given for this choice — to be more available, for the Kingdom, to love everyone and not just one person — sometimes don't make much sense. There's no best way to be a sexual person. What tyranny we suffer early in life by believing that we must be other than who we are. By mid-life I came home to the fact that, when all was said and done, celibate and chaste was my best way. Had I chosen otherwise, I wouldn't be myself.

Two, the labels — normal and not — rarely ever help you. By forty-six I'd had my fill of them. What a relief to admit that they were no longer of any use to me. I asked myself: "Why follow someone else's formula for what I should or should not feel?" — and promised not to try. I am better now at accepting and cherishing all my feelings — and withholding any judgments, too. Life is much too short to worry unduly what others may think; why wait until eighty to be myself?

Three, sexuality and spirituality are best friends, not foes. Wasn't it God, after all, who passed out sexual energy — maybe just to get my notice. By mid-life I realized that sexual and spiritual energy had a place in every great relationship of mine. Where spirituality was lacking, lust often enough made its home. And when sexual energy could not be found, I had a relationship on my hands that lacked something very human.

Most importantly, though, sickness and its remedy reminded me that relationships will count for a great deal when mid-life sexuality is reviewed for the final time. Those links we have with others, and with God, and with ourselves. After forty, though, isn't it intimacy that we seek — the simple exchange of love and vulnerabilities?

A few times in life I've been in love — that intoxicating, maddening, all consuming type that makes sleep both unnecessary and impossible at the same time. At mid-life who among us does not long for this type of passion? We all want someone or something over which to lose sleep again, a passion that will focus and take us well beyond ourselves. Mid-life sexuality teaches us this important lesson well: to be happy during life's afternoon — if you have not already done so — you must find your passion and give yourself to it. By age fifty we must commit to something larger than ourselves.

At mid-life there is also that growing urgency we feel to pass life along. It helped me to remember that early in life it is important for some of us to conceive a child. By forty-seven, however, I no longer yearned for children of my own, and realized, instead, that there was parenting enough to do without adding to the population. The next generation and those who will follow are now my concern. A tender care has grown in me for those beginning to make their way in life — a desire has risen up to mentor and, perhaps, leave a lasting legacy.

In retrospect I'm not surprised that mid-life illness and its cure helped me be more at home with sex and sexuality. All the adolescent urgency that so preoccupied me at fourteen returned and took me on a fast forward trip through my sexual history. This time around, however, the terrain was familiar, and I saw it all with clearer eyes. After all, to be fourteen at forty-six, you must also quickly be twenty and thirty-four again.

I will never equate mid-life sexuality with waning energy or lack of it. One of its first fruits is a wonderful sense of being alive. I know it brought me to life in ways I had not known before. My longings are now less predictable and self-involved, more nurturing, other-directed and, quite frankly, fun.

So much of life is taken up with searching out where we need to be. At forty-seven, happy to be sexually alive, I rest contented that I am where I need to be. I continue to live this life of celibate chastity — yes, it's my way of being a sexual person. Each morning, though, I must refresh that commitment, but can't we all say the very same thing?

Each month begins with a testosterone treatment — 250 c.c.'s. Two years ago at the start of this regimen, my doctor asked, "Any reactions?" "Yes," I responded, "I feel as if I'm sixteen again!" Puzzled, she replied, "Sixteen, don't you mean thirteen or fourteen?" Thought I, "That's right, by sixteen I had discovered guilt!" Each month's initial jolt reminds me, once again, that, yes, it can be fun to feel like fourteen or sixteen from time to time. I am also reassured, however, that mid-life is a much greater blessing. The difference? Here at almost forty-eight, I think I am safe in saying that there is, at least, some wisdom in the soup.

CHAPTER VIII

COPING WITH THE
TRANSITION AT MID-LIFE

*B*y this point in our story about
mid-life, hopefully we can agree that it is a challenging time in
life. There are, however, many ways to cope with the developmental tasks that present themselves during this period and the
years that follow. This chapter examines some of the means
available for managing change at mid-life — those that work
well, and some that are a "dead-end-street."

Change is difficult for most of us. In our attempt to deal
with it at mid-life, some of us deny that any change is taking
place. Others of us hope that rearranging a few externals will
guarantee that all will be well. Neither approach to change is
helpful.

Before examining a few genuine ways of coping with transitions, we will discuss two false interventions: the workshop
high and the geographical cure. Both are similar to medical
treatment that relieves the symptoms of a disease but does little
to alter its natural course.

FALSE INTERVENTIONS

For some of us the solution to many of life's challenges and problems is found by attending a workshop. Although these gatherings can be useful learning tools, they are not a panacea. For many of us, though, a workshop is like a "fix." We return from it with momentary good feelings, but quickly find that the same problems and difficulties remain.

At the very least, a workshop is like a paid vacation. As it winds down we can say, "It was fun meeting people there and the person running it was quite good." Workshops, however, need to be used as they were intended: to provide some useful information and to allow us an opportunity to meet others facing the same challenges and difficulties. They cannot act as a substitute for the hard developmental work of a life transition.

The geographical cure, a second false intervention, is rooted in the belief that our difficulties have very little to do with us but rather result from external causes. In attempting to solve problems, therefore, we first consider changing locations or, more often, careers, relationships, lifestyles, and commitments. The comments of a recently divorced middle-aged man illustrate the fallacy of such quick solutions. "Sometimes I fantasize," he quipped, "about hopping on a plane to South America and starting a whole new life, but the trouble is that I know I'd be waiting for me when I got off the plane." At mid-life, it will do little good to change our external situation without also changing ourselves.

Both of these solutions to the pressures of the mid-life or any transition have a magical aura about them. We all look for simple solutions to complex problems and hope that by performing certain activities, we will work magical changes in ourselves. The user of any "magic wand" solution, of course, also believes that change should be instant and painless. Belief in magic dies hard. At mid-life and on into the later years of life, many of us persist in seeking unrealistic solutions to transitional dilemmas. Even when our solutions are ineffectual, rather than accepting the fact that a magical solution has failed, we believe instead that the correct magical solution has not yet been found. So, the search continues.

HELPFUL WAYS OF COPING AT MID-LIFE

Genuine and helpful ways of coping with change take time, effort, perseverance. Several are worthy of mention. To begin with, *we can take seriously the transition at mid-life and others we encounter in life, and recognize their characteristic shape.* Each includes a time of disintegration during which an old order comes to an end. This first phase is followed by a span of fertile emptiness during which fruitful reevaluation and change can take place. Finally, a new beginning gets underway.

Human growth is a messy business, so *try to imagine the course of life as a ripening. Each season has its place and purpose.* Although we may wonder if some will ever end, we do well to remember this fact: the spring would not be half so welcomed if we lacked the storms and cold of winter.

Second, *we must learn to take our time during life transitions.* The developmental work of mid-life cannot be hurried. It is not finished in a week, a month, or even a year, but rather takes about four to five years on the average. In addition to bringing a chapter of our life to a close, we need to discover what it is we must learn for the next step we are going to take. Premature action will abort this process.

Third, during any life transition, *it is better to avoid acting for the sake of action.* Activity of this type can sometimes be an attempt to avoid the pain of growth. If we blame our discomfort on those with whom we live or work, our life commitments, the success of others — almost anything but ourselves and the change taking place in our life — we run the risk of rearranging externals without also changing ourselves. Stated simply: we pave the way for the "geographical cure."

Fourth, *we can recognize our need to mourn at mid-life.* We have to evaluate not only the person that we have become but must also mourn those parts of our personalities that we were unable to develop because of past decisions. The religious priest who will now never be a father, the businessman who chose to forego a career in education for life in the corporate world, parents who decided to develop a relationship with their family rather than a talent or interest of their own — all these men and women need to mourn those lost parts of themselves.

Fifth, *goals and values can be reexamined during a period of transition.* We can use the time as an impetus for a new kind of learning about ourselves and for examining what we hold to be important. We can facilitate this process by planning some idleness in our day, having a retreat space at home, or restructuring trips and vacations so that we attain much needed leisure.

Sixth, *we can learn to become mentors.* In assisting others to identify their Dream and give it a place in their life, we leave a living legacy, one more lasting than brick and stone. At mid-life let's heed this advice of Goethe in our own life and pass it along to others: "What you can do, or dream you can do, begin it. Boldness has genius, power, and magic in it." Be a mentor!

Seventh, during any transitional time *resist the pressure to conform.* If we take the mid-life transition seriously, for example, others will often be frightened. Moreover, those of us who attempt a radical critique of ourselves and our lives will encounter strong resistance from parts of ourselves and from other people. It is important to resist the pressure to get back into step. Thoreau said it best: "If a man does not keep pace with his companions, perhaps it is because he hears a different drummer. Let him step to the music which he hears, however measured or far away." Mid-life is the time to heed this advice; step to it.

Eighth, at mid-life, as during any time of transition, *we all need someone with whom to talk.* Be it a good friend, a counselor or mental health professional, or a spiritual guide, we can benefit from someone who helps us put our life dilemmas and feelings into words so as to understand them better.

Finally, *we can take care of ourselves in small ways.* An example? A fifty-year-old married woman reports that every morning she rises before the other members of her family so as to make the "perfect cup of coffee." And what constitutes the "perfect cup of coffee"? *Coffee exactly the way she likes it!* During any transition we are pushed, pulled, squeezed, and stretched. Taking care of ourselves during times of life change, or at any time for that matter, is not an indication of a selfish nature. Rather, it demonstrates healthy self-respect.

Development during the adult years, then, can take us home to that genuine self that lives within us all. Mid-life, in particular, is a central part of this pilgrimage toward what is deepest and best within each of us. It can leave us whole, better integrated, spiritually alive, and more life-giving men and women. Such maturity does not come cheaply, however, but is worth every combined ounce of human effort and divine grace. In the end, mid-life and its transition can be the harbinger of a second springtime — one that blossoms into the glorious summer and autumn harvest of later life.

<u>REFLECTION QUESTION</u>

Take a few minutes to consider the following reflection question and to jot down a few personal notes for later reflection.

1. What means of coping with the transition at mid-life make most sense to you? Spend some time developing your own personal "Coping Plan" for mid-life and its aftermath.

CHAPTER IX

MID-LIFE ATHLETE

*A*t mid-life I became an athlete —
by mistake. By mistake and not through any infusion of natural talent or years of disciplined practice. At forty-seven, somehow, this boyhood klutz — last chosen for most teams — began to shine.

I've always been mistaken for an athlete. A year ago, for example, a young man by the name of Kirk — a natural athlete, I'd say — inquired whether tennis was my game; and if so, how about a match. I smiled with pleasure but begged off. "No, I'm not the 'tennis type,'" I said, failing to confess that I had never found the secret of connecting the racquet with the ball.

In another example — at least ten years ago — I foolishly agreed to join a colleague at the gym for a game of racquet ball. Another case of mistaken identity. Full of myself, I bought the shoes, a racquet, and a can of balls. The outcome of our match? He "wiped the court with me." I managed, "You've played before?" "Yes, intercollegiately," came the reply. It was our first and last game. I have the racquet still; it's almost new, used only once, of course.

I've been mistaken for the tennis type, a racquet ball aficionado, and also for a sailor, an equestrian, a mountaineer, and so much more. In recent years — in the midst of long cross country runs — strangers half my age invite me to join their pickup games of football. I manage to beg off gracefully. While flattered, no longer am I foolish enough to mix it up with those I could have sired.

What lies behind this case of mistaken identity? After all, the sportsman of my youth was quite a dud indeed, always last chosen for any team. Though most often assigned eventually to one side or the other, I knew full well that my mates saw me as a liability. How could they not — I saw myself that way too. Being picked last for a team — it's like going to an auction where everything is really free. The gavel's thud is but a ruse; no money will ever exchange hands. The sportsman of my boyhood often found himself left behind — unpurchased — when all the bidding was done. He couldn't even be given away.

Be last chosen for any team as a boy and you'll take with you to life's later years the same picture album of memories that I did. Bases loaded, two out, you step up to the plate. First you hear the groans, next you see the action: fellow team mates, gloves in hand, ready themselves to return to the field. All this before the first pitch is thrown! You get over it, of course, and insist it's history — until you see another boy just starting out in life left on the sidelines after the choice for teams is made.

What happened at forty-seven to bring the athlete in me to life? I bought myself a pair of running shoes and swimming trunks, and agreed to live by these simple instructions: don't wear the two at the same time. More importantly, the sportsman in me woke up because mid-life taught me how to play. A perennially slow learner, I finally mastered this important lesson: "Why compete when you can just as well have fun."

I take little advice about my sporting life these days. Yes, I read all the books and listen to endless tales about individual feats of heroism during the Bay to Breakers or on "Heartbreak Hill" in Boston each Patriots' Day. Not for me, I say. When tired, I stop; when frisky, I run or swim. I relish quiet country roads where I can plod along — alone, content to set my pace and run in my own way and at my own speed.

Of late, though, I've noticed one unwelcome change. Injuries — those dreaded trophies of all mid-life athletes — have come my way more often than before. They are awarded, too, at the most inopportune of times: in the middle of a run. Consulting a physiotherapist, I was given this sage advice: "At your age, you must stretch more." "At your age, why not consider running a half hour in the morning and another in the evening, rather than an hour all at once?" "At your age, you might consider another sport, like walking!"

Why does that phrase, "at your age" always seems to stick? Perhaps because of the unspoken advice that follows — "At your age, you should know better!" When you have been born again to the sporting life in middle age, however, you don't lose faith so easily. Instead, you realize that it's best to stretch more, and — yes — run a half hour in the morning and another at day's end. As for switching to walking — well, let's leave that for another lifetime.

A friend also offered this counsel, "At our age we must come back slowly from an injury. Sometimes it takes twice or three times as long to regain the conditioning we had." Some days it is difficult to realize that you are at that age about which everyone speaks so reverently. Thoughts of coming back slowly are the farthest thing from mind.

Such was the case during a mid-morning run in Bordeaux. The day? Crisp, clear, the kind that makes you want to keep on moving forever. Entering the park and starting my workout, I spied a young man moving along slowly; his age — early twenties. I thought to myself, "My pace-setter," and ran to catch up. Hearing me approach, he looked back, curious as to who was behind; a smile and then we loped along for another twenty minutes.

As we moved over trail and later lawn, dodging sprinklers that sputtered suddenly to life, I found myself musing: "This young man would be the age of my son, had I a son." I began to wonder what this now never to be son would be like, how he'd look, what he'd believe, whether he'd want me for a friend here at almost fifty. My reverie ended quickly as I discovered that my running mate — the one I thought was setting pace for me — was really using me for warming up himself. When a contemporary flashed by, he was off quickly in hot pursuit.

I continued to lumber along slowly, making my rounds, being careful not to strain any of three recent injuries. And I must confess, I also wondered: "Will the rest of life be made up of 'coming back slowly from injuries!'"

But don't believe those pundits who insist that our bodies don't work so well at mid-life as they did before. They just work differently and demand a bit more care. If you listen carefully to the rhythm and the mood of yours, you too can be a mid-life athlete. I recommend it highly. You will feel more alive, content and come to know yourself in a brand new way.

When in the local park in recent months I no longer set my pace by the twenty-year-olds who share the track with me. I also fail to be insulted when I realize that some use my speed bursts to warm themselves for the run that lies ahead. I stop when tired, walk when a muscle pulls, and apply ice in a timely fashion when my age escapes me for a while.

The rewards of sport at forty-seven are great. They include those moments that would feed the ego of any self-respecting athlete, but are especially nourishing to the mid-life soul. Before the sun has risen, for example, I have been applauded enthusiastically — during my morning jog to nowhere in particular

— by cheering Chinese children gathered in Tienneman for the daily raising of the flag. Tiny Japanese boys and girls have also run along side chirping "arro," "arro" before collapsing into that explosive way of laughing children have — the one that makes them look as though they will burst if they do not quickly find a way to release all their pent-up air.

Many people tell me that they wonder why — with all that must be done each day — I take an hour to run along going absolutely nowhere and with no apparent purpose. Isn't that the secret, though, of all real mid-life athletes? We like it best when there is no purpose but having fun. To be a child at mid-life is another way of reinventing yourself.

By the way, that young man — the twenty-something-year-old — the one in Bordeaux who set his pace by me and then took off, leaving me to plod along? Well, I caught up with him — eventually. And, believe it or not, bested him in the end. No competition. Mid-life, indeed!

Reflection Question

1. Write your own mid-life essay. Pick a theme: mortality, friendship, aging, the freedom that comes with forty or fifty, sexuality, spirituality — any theme — and write about your mid-life experience.

EPILOGUE

We buried James this morning. His age? Fifty something. The cause of death? "He was always sickly," I was told. James was a leper — a strange way to introduce anyone, I know, but, with James, it was always the first thing anyone told me about him. He lived here at the "Nike Centre for Cured Lepers" — Enugu, Nigeria. No one wants these folks; I guess most people are afraid that "cured leper" is a misnomer.

Death came for James late last night. By daybreak final preparations for his burial were complete. Standing in the doorway of his room at mid-morning, with his body being prepared for burial, I was aware that the odor of death already hung in the air. The heat in this part of the world insured that such was the case. Months ago, when Descarga brought back from Rwanda the few personal effects of Chris and Joseph — items that had been found next to the bodies in the car — this smell was there too. You cannot mistake it, or shake it off either — it stays with you. This morning I knew all would be accomplished quickly within a few hours of James's passing.

One of the local tribesmen built his casket, asking only a bottle of Coke as payment. A simple affair made from scraps of wood. Others dug the grave, up there on the hill amidst the tall grass. When the time came, fellow residents of the Centre lined the box with James' clothing, lifted his body from the bed — already stiff, his hands and feet tied with gauze, cotton wool spilling out of his mouth and nose, his eyes open, hollow and blank — and placed it in the casket. Yes, he was very dead.

I thought to myself, "Isn't this how it will end for us all." No matter our station in life nor how elaborately a culture attempts to disguise the fact that we are dead, in the end — if we are lucky — it comes down to these realities: a box, a place in the earth for our remains, a few prayers, and — sometimes — the grief of others. Then, life moves on. It all happens very quickly, in a flash, once only. For James, there wasn't even the consolation of family; no one wanted him. His blood relations had refused to see him; not even an inquiry about his well-being in forty-eight months.

I didn't know James personally, and as I looked around the room where he had spent so many years of his life, I wondered what his journey had been like. Whom did he love, who loved him, did he have any dreams and hopes near the end, what made him laugh or cry? The room had a disordered tidiness about it, "It's much like my own," I thought. When you are dying, though, you don't give much concern to order and cleanliness.

Burying the dead — it is one of mid-life's chores. You do it, you mourn, but then you must get on with life. Later I saw the mourners carrying palm wine down to the area where the residents live. They say that the Igbos are the "Irish of Africa." Yes, I told myself, right down to the grog after the burial!

Later in the day I went for a run. The weather sultry, a storm trying to get up a head of steam — sputtering now and then to remind me of its presence. The time: day's end with many people walking the road, heading home; as always, the children chanting, "White man, white man." Everyone is so welcoming here, the scenery sensuous and lush. What a contrast to the morning and its tasks!

As I headed up a hill, I felt a stream of cool air wash over me, even as my lungs began to burn. Some children ran alongside, laughing and pushing as children always seem to do. I thought of James, here in this place brimming with life. Had he ever wanted to run like this, be greeted by strangers, gawked at by children — he probably had a lot of the latter in his days, but not the kind of gawking he wished or I get.

There has been a lot of dying in my life of late; now it is time to get on with living again. I hope this book has helped you to see that mid-life is a passage to something better, richer, freer, and more in keeping with what our God wanted in the first place. About age forty we begin to let go and in so doing start to find our real selves. What a blessing! I'm glad I'm almost fifty and hope for many years beyond that milestone. It is good to be alive, to breathe fresh air, to love some people and a God who asks only that I be myself, to have a purpose, to savor a few very simple things in life.

I turned on the road and headed home. James's death, the heat of the day, the cleansing sweat of my run, the welcoming faces of so many, the contrast of rich and poor in this part of the world — all reminded me of the complexity of life in recent years and also of its utter simplicity. On the way back I stopped to help some young men push a van that had stalled. As we grunted and strained and talked, I thought: "What satisfaction to feel young in a brand new way, strong and seasoned at the very same time, hopeful, connected." Afterwards, I took up my run once again; a short way down the road I jumped to touch the hanging branch of a tree and to shoot a few imaginary hoops! Yes, I thought, at mid-life it's a gift to run, and to jump, and to shoot!

Sean D. Sammon, FMS
Nike Centre
Enugu, Nigeria
24 August 1995

RECOMMENDED READINGS

Bridges, William. *Transitions.* Reading, MA: Addison-Wesley, 1980.

Sammon, Sean D. *An Undivided Heart: Making Sense of Celibate Chastity.* Staten Island, NY: Alba House, 1993.

Sammon, Sean D. *Growing Pains in Ministry.* Whitinsville, MA: Affirmation Books, 1983. (Available from Twenty-Third Publications, Mystic, CT).

Sammon, Sean D. "Life After Youth," *Human Development,* Spring 1982.

Sellner, Edward. *Mentoring: The Ministry of Spiritual Kinship.* Notre Dame, IN: Ave Maria Press, 1990.

Sheehy, Gail. *New Passages: Mapping Your Life Across Time.* New York, NY: Random House, 1995.

Sheehy, Gail. *The Silent Passage.* New York, NY: Random House, 1992.

Whitehead, Evelyn E. and James D. *Christian Life Patterns.* New York, NY: Doubleday, 1979.

Whitehead, Evelyn E. and James D. *Seasons of Strength.* New York, NY: Doubleday, 1983.